DIGGING FOR
TREASURE

DIGGING FOR
TREASURE

A Guide to Finding Valuable
Victorian Rubbish Dumps

Ron Dale

ISBN: Softcover   978-1-4797-1476-6
               Ebook   978-1-4797-1477-3

This book was printed in the United States of America.

To order additional copies of this book, contact:
Xlibris Corporation
0-800-644-6988
www.xlibrispublishing.co.uk
Orders@xlibrispublishing.co.uk
304918

CONTENTS

INTRODUCTION

ALLOW ME TO INTRODUCE MYSELF:

In the 1970s and 80s I spent over 10 years digging full-time into Victorian and Edwardian rubbish dumps and for several years after this it was also my part-time hobby. Additionally, I was running a Sunday auction at Hollingbourne in Kent for the finds: antique bottles and printed pot-lids, dolls heads and salt-glazed stoneware. I also sold my own finds to collectors and dealers from all over the world at a stall in the famous Bermondsey Antique Market in Long Lane, London and Maidstone market in Kent.

In my spare time I also wrote magazine articles, resulting from my own research, as dump-digging was in its infancy in the early 70s and there was no published information on the finds. These were published in a variety of magazines such as *Treasure Hunting, Kollectorama, Bottles & Relics News, Antique Bottle Collecting, Art & Antiques Weekly, The Lady* and many others. In 1977 I was able to publish a comprehensive book, *The Price Guide to Black & White Pot-Lids* through the Antique Collectors Club of Woodbridge, illustrating over 2,300 different advertising pot-lids with their approximate dates and values. This was only made possible due to the flow of pot-lids through my auctions which at this time were the only ones existing in the U.K. for dump finds as they are called today. This book was the very first price guide on these types of advertising lids and has since become a classic in its own right, being something of a collector's item itself. Although a revised paperback edition was published in 1987, the values quoted in this are long out-of-date and more up-to-date valuation guides for some lids now exist. However, it still stands alone as the most comprehensive listing of pot-lids between two covers. There is breaking news of a soon-to-be-published book of pot-lids listing 7,000, which shoots mine out of the water. This is good news as research should be progressive and such a book is long overdue and I am looking forward to seeing what has been found since 1977. It is time all these newly-discovered lids were between the covers of one large book and values updated. Since those early days advertising pot-lids have escalated enormously in value and are still keenly sought by collectors in all parts of the world, many of them realising from £200 to £300 each and the very rare reaching up to £5,000. Not a bad price for an old hair grease, toothpaste or fish paste lid thrown away in someone's dustbin just over a century ago! It seems natural that the value of bottles I was digging out in the 1970s have increased and I have been surprised to see many printed ginger beer bottles commanding as much as £40 to £80 each for the rarer pictorial specimens. I remember well finding the first blue submarine poison bottles in the 1970s and seeing them sell for £5 to £8 each in my auctions, but although they were not common in those days, we were pleased to accept such prices. Today they sell from £800 to over £1,000 each. It is encouraging to me as an "old-timer," to see that a hobby which I participated in at the very beginning of an exciting time is still flourishing. The fact is that in the early 1970s no-one alive could remember the pot-lids and bottles we were finding from the 19th century. They had been thrown away, buried and forgotten. Then along we came and dug them up to start a new hobby, and an interesting one at that. Digging outside in the fresh air is good exercise, healthy and profitable. Furthermore it's exciting as you never know what rarity you might find on the next shovelful and although in those early days there was no fixed price range as we did not know what was rare and what was not, prices have eventually found their own levels like water does.

The hobby of digging century-old rubbish dumps and collecting the finds has mushroomed enormously since I first started digging and it is now well established in the U.K., Australia, New Zealand and in the

U.S.A. Although my experience of digging has been only in the U.K., the principles of finding dumps applies equally to all countries of the world as all houses and farms built before about 1880 would have their own rubbish dump with valuable finds still buried underground, waiting for someone to dig up this forgotten treasure.

I have heard it said that all British dumps are now dug out. Nonsense! My gazetteer of 1904 lists over 50,000 towns and villages in the U.K. and I am absolutely certain this number of dumps or even half that number have not been found from Victorian and Edwardian times. Read on and I will tell you why.

I will also advise you how to find these valuable early rubbish dumps. I am no longer able to do such physical work, having developed a spinal problem and having reached the tender age of 80, I think I have to hang up my digging fork. I hope to pass on to another generation the enthusiasm for dump-digging—the thrill of finding rarities—the gaining of a new hobby in which all the family can participate. Now you know who I am and that (like Oscar Wilde) I wish to remind people that rumours of my death are exaggerated. Please allow me to introduce you to the world of dump-digging, to the treasures hidden under the ground for over a century. And although the finds are not gold coins, they are treasure in other ways: they do have a cash value, but digging for dump relics is not all about money. You will never get rich from dump-digging. It is more about finding something with a garden fork and spade which was discarded as useless by previous generations and today may be regarded in a different light. It is about finding antiques which did not exist to be seen anywhere on earth, because they were buried under the ground. It is about digging up your own antiques. There is a thrill in re-discovering such items from a previous century. And the finds themselves—lowly household containers of no interest in the 19th century—have since acquired charm, antiquity and in some instances a high value. Also there is beauty in the colours of deep cobalt blue poison bottles, the antique mottled surface of a bitters bottle reflecting the wooden mould into which it may have been mouth-blown and the striations in a bottle-neck caused when an apprentice applied a lip by hand-tools to a crude jagged bottle-top. And there is the printed humour of the advertising on certain ointment pots claiming they could cure gout, rheumatism, erysipelas, myxomatosis, galloping lugrot, the screaming heebygeebees etc. Personally, I also find the diversity of typography on Victorian pot-lid advertising to be fascinating too as some used several fonts on the same lid to attract attention. The finds in old dumps may not have the value of gold, weight for weight (although some do), but in more than one way they are treasures and a new-found dump can be worth many thousands of pounds. *What better hobby could you ask for than to be able to dig up your own antiques from out of the ground?* And you do not have to declare them as treasure trove!

To the seasoned dump-digger who might wish to read these outpourings of mine for the sake of curiosity: I cannot teach you to suck eggs, but perhaps you might just enjoy re-living some of my experiences of the past; and you just never know, you may possibly learn a wrinkle or two!

I am already feeling nostalgic about the days, the months and years I enjoyed digging for treasure, but I have had my time. Now it is your turn. Please don't waste it. Time passes quicker as you age.

CHAPTER ONE

The Beginnings of Refuse Collection

I have heard it said many times, "*There's nowhere left to dig today. All the dumps have been found and dug out.*" To coin a phrase, I say, "*Rubbish.*"

Before proceeding to search for dumps it will be useful to take a quick look at the history of refuse collection, which is what I did after I discovered my first Victorian dump in the early 1970s. We need not be impatient. The unfound dumps out there have been unfound for a century or more and are not going to disappear overnight. The obvious dumps may have been found already; the others can only be found by those who study how to find them. Many diggers gravitate towards ancient towns in their search for old rubbish dumps in the mistaken and naive belief that these will have the most ancient dumps. Not true! The age or history of a town or village has no bearing on the age of its dump. There was no collection of refuse in the 17th or 18th century. Nor was there any in the first three-quarters of the 19th century, except in London, so please don't expect to find any from these early dates. (But see later chapter on private country house dumps).

The organised dumping of household refuse collected from houses in the U.K. began in London about the 1870s onwards, in large towns about 1880 and in small towns and villages from 1900, but in some rural areas as late as 1920. In London there was a collection business ran by companies called scavenger companies which operated prior to 1870 (but *only* in London). However this early collection of refuse was not dumped. It was recycled. The companies used to tender to each individual London council to pay for the right to collect the rubbish. The reason for this was that in London it had a recycle value. This was the reason for the first collecting of refuse—not for reasons of hygiene—but to make a profit for the scavenger companies who were, in fact, the first recyclers. They not only sold off the coal ash in the refuse; they also sold practically everything else. At this time most houses used coal for heating and baking and we did not have the variety or volume of packaging we have today. Paper would be re-used to light fires, many glass bottles were re-used and could be sold back to the glass companies; stoneware jars and pots were sometimes thrown out, but many were re-used for storage for jams and other preserves. Although cans were in use in mid-Victorian times, there were not so many canned products and there were certainly no plastic containers. If you were to examine the contents of a Victorian dustbin, as all dump-diggers do, you would find a wide variety of glass bottles, many brown salt-glazed stoneware jars, printed ceramic lids and pots for cold cream, shaving cream, lip salve, bears grease pomade, bloater paste and other products. Jam and marmalade came in white or cream-glazed jars and blacking for boots and cast-iron fireplaces was sold in brown salt-glazed stoneware jars. Dolly-blue (Giessen Blue) or blueing for whitening the washing was sold in small cylindrical brown stone bottles and these are naturally found in large numbers. Ink came in both glass and stone bottles in a wide variety of shapes and colours, all collectable. Quack medicines came in embossed glass bottles and are keenly sought by collectors all over the world. Due to the fact that many people were illiterate in the 1800s, bottles containing poisonous substances for external use only, such as liniments, were made with ridges and grooves on them in addition to the words "poison" or "poisonous," so that even in the poor light of an oil lamp, they could be identified by touch even by an illiterate person. They were first produced in attractive cobalt blue glass bottles as a warning that blue meant danger and the dark glass also prevented sunlight from affecting the contents. Many accidental poisonings had occurred prior to this but the addition of cobalt to the glass bottles increased the cost and unusual examples of these are highly-prized. When I first dug up the rugby-ball shaped poison bottles about 1970, they reminded me of a miniature submarine (see illustration) and thereafter I called them submarine poisons in my writing and in the auctions. They are now very rare. You would also find (after about 1880) many short dumpy brown-glass Bovril bottles which are very common, followed by their many imitators. When children's dolls had broken bodies, they were thrown away complete with their bisque porcelain heads or the smaller glazed head and shoulders and these are keenly sought today in good condition to re-make old dolls. Lastly, you will always find clay pipes, mainly with broken stems, often with a pictorial device on the bowl signifying the name of the pub or club which supplied them to customers. All such items are collected today and even though many are common and have a low value, it is the uncommon ones which, if attractive, attain high prices. But the main ingredient in any Victorian dustbin would be coal ash and this too had a value to brick-makers and others.

Before refuse was dumped in London, it was sold to the scavenger companies for a high price for complete recycling. Every year on a certain day these companies were invited to submit tenders to the vestry of the parish, offering their bid. Those who offered the highest price gained the contract. As an example: in 1846 the Court of Sewers in London was paid £5,000 by the contractors for the privilege of emptying the dustbins and clearing rubbish off the streets. In addition to recycling it, there was a huge international demand for household rubbish. Auctions were held on board the Thames barges which transported it and boatloads of dustbin rubbish arrived in London every day, mainly from Newcastle and other northern ports. It sold for about 15s. to £1 per chaldron (1.309 cubic metres) One of the reasons for its great demand was that much land was being reclaimed from the sea at this time, both in Britain and on the Continent. With the Repeal of the Corn Laws, farmers were hungry for land and land reclamation became popular. Swampy lands and heavy clay soils needed something to turn it into friable growing soil and coal ash, high in nutrients was used. Somewhere, perhaps in Holland, France or Belgium, lie buried under farmland many tons of early Victorian rubbish and its relics.

Where the refuse was recycled in England the dustbins were emptied by horse and carts and taken to a large sorting yard. The average yard in London employed between thirty and forty people, but the largest, near Regents Park, employed over 120 people by 1850. The main demand for the fine, gritty ash was used for improving heavy clay soils on farmland and for making bricks. It was mixed in with the pug clay to make firm bricks. Fleets of brickworks spritsail barges continuously plied the Thames and Medway rivers, bringing bricks to London and returning laden with household refuse, bought in the auctions to deliver to the numerous brickworks on the river banks of the Medway in Kent and the Thames in south Essex.

In time, the contractors—nearly 100 of them in London—banded together and decided not to offer so much when bidding. By applying this "ringing" of their bids, they were in time able to get the refuse for practically nothing. These companies were operated by businessmen out to make a profit from the recycling of household refuse, mainly from the coal ash. They were often called "dust contractors" and they supplied the men and the horses and carts to collect it. For many years in the 1840s up to the 1860s they took it to recycling yards, the large one on the banks of the Regents Canal in London was described by Henry Mayhew in his study of the working class, *London Labour and the London Poor* of 1851.

In these sorting yards whole families worked: men, their wives and often their children. They would sometimes be accompanied by their dogs (to feed on free meat-bones), chickens and pigs were kept to gobble up any food-waste. Horse and carts would be arriving, unloading all day long. There would be clouds of ash blowing around. The scene would be one of muck and dust, stench and noise. But oh what I would give to be able to travel back in time to be there and help them sort the rubbish! Horse manure from the streets was mixed with manure from their pigs and chickens and sold to make Giessen blue, often known later as dolly-blue for whitening the washing as it contained ammonia. The women sorted out many smaller items from the refuse. Oyster shells were sold to cutlery manufacturers who used the mother-of-pearl for handles; bricks and brickbats were sold for laying road foundations; bones were converted into glue or fertiliser; old cans were sold for making the japanned corners of wooden cabin trunks; old boots and shoes were sold to shoemakers who used the old leather to layer between the inner and outer soles; glass bottles were sold back to their makers and had a value of 3d per dozen for wine, beer and mineral waters; rags went to make fertiliser, glue or paper; all kinds of metal was sold to specialist scrap metal dealers. Broken glass was sold as cullet for re-melting (as it is today). Even the rotting cabbage leaves and potato peelings were eaten by the pigs which were eventually eaten themselves. One of the most valuable contents was the ash and this was sold for a variety of purposes. Nothing was wasted except the finest of dust which blew across the Regents Canal on windy days. This was recycling at its peak.

Later, due to a variety of reasons, the second-hand value of refuse dropped. It was no longer profitable to recycle it and the situation was reversed. The main cause was probably mass production methods when machinery came into use. If the dust contractors did not wish to buy it, the councils then had to pay them to take it away and dump it. This is where the history of refuse becomes of more significance to us, as it was then dumped commercially for the very first time. There was one exception to all this re-cycling and that is the material bought by the Kent and South Essex brickworks on whose land I did most of my years of digging. The unsorted refuse bought for making bricks was known as "rough stuff." It was unsorted refuse containing bottles, pot-lids, jars and broken material of all kind, but it still contained the fine ash needed for brick-making. Brickworks dumps will be discussed in a later chapter.

In other cities and large towns, around 1880 the collection, emptying of dustbins throughout the country began, not obviously all at the same time. Smaller towns and villages had to wait another twenty or thirty years before refuse collection began. And in small villages the first organised collection could be as late as 1910 to 1920 even.

The obvious question is: *what happened to domestic waste before there was any council collection?* I'm glad you asked me that. It was simply thrown away over the bottom fence of the garden, in the nearest woods, rivers or streams. Or you had to pay someone to take it and dump it for you. As I have mentioned, the poor would not have had much packaging refuse and what they could re-sell they did. They could resell glass bottles at the local chandler's shops and even stoneware pots had a small value. Many poor people made a living selling ginger-beer in parks and street corners from a barrow. They made the drink in their back yards and there was a demand for second-hand plain ginger-beer bottles. Even when I was young in the 1930s and 40s, glass lemonade bottles were taken back to the shops to claim half-a-penny or a penny on the quart sizes. Some families discarded them in the dustbin and we kids had great fun searching for them on the dump at the weekend and washing them clean in the river. We often made more money than our weekly allowance this way. We can see, therefore, that the waste from poor families in Victorian times was minimal. The majority of dumps I have encountered date from the period 1880 to 1920, although I have occasionally dug 1920s or 30s dumps if I happened to encounter them as they can yield finds not dug in older sites, but they are definitely less profitable, containing hardly any pot-lids which had been made obsolete by the introduction of the squeezable toothpaste tube in the U.S. around the First World War period. Prior to this invention, some chemists made their own toothpaste, cold cream etc. and sold it in small ceramic pots. The lids were often transfer-printed with advertising of their own choice and printed under the glaze. These are the lids which today are collected and coveted.

In Leeds, Yorkshire, refuse was incinerated in the 1880s in gigantic furnaces and the ash from these was used to make fertiliser and cement. There would therefore be few pot-lids and bottles from the 1880s dumped in this large northern city. In all parts of the country councils did not always just have one dump. Often it was used for projects such as infilling quarries, land reclamation from the sea and by builders of roads. I know of one small village in Northamptonshire where the main road into the village is about twenty-feet higher than the surrounding land on one side and certain people dug into its sloping banks once or twice, as it was all valuable refuse containing dark green Codd bottles worth about £10 each at that time. You could earn £100 a night there with a strong torch and that was over 30 years ago. The police were called in to discourage the digging before the main road collapsed! I can't remember the name of the village. Your memory diminishes as you age. But of course, I wasn't there, was I? In a town near where I live, I know of a road bridge over the mainline railway line that is shored up by local Edwardian refuse, but digging is strictly not allowed there.

Why are old bottles interesting and valuable? Are they different from modern bottles and why? Readers who have not encountered old bottles and pot-lids yet will obviously wonder what the attraction is. Here, a brief explanation may be helpful for newcomers to the hobby. Up to about the First World War, all bottles were blown by glass-blowers individually into a mould. The top of the bottle was then quickly cut off with a pair of shears, leaving a jagged top. Then an apprentice quickly applied a smooth lip to this jagged top on drink bottles, e.g. beer, wine etc. On cheap ink bottles this was left jagged as drinking ink was not popular at this time. A full bottle of ink cost only a penny and it is their very crudity which is interesting. Some of these inks are crammed with hundreds of tiny air bubbles, trapped for eternity inside a humble penny ink bottle. Sometimes the neck of an old hock bottle has striations in it, showing a left-hand twist or a right-hand twist, reflecting the direction the blower turned the bottle when the lip was being applied. And because hock bottles were often used on the table, the seams were ground off to produce an elegant tapering bottle in many different hues of blue green and amber. Because they were mouth-blown and had to be physically handled, the thickness of old wine, beer and pop bottles is three times the thickness of a modern bottle. Also, as the glassblower drew off the glass from the top of a cauldron of bubbling molten glass, when he blew the glass, air bubbles were trapped inside the glass and these can often be seen in many old bottles. When the A.B.M. was invented (automatic blowing machine) and introduced around the time of the First World War (a gradual process), bottles were then machine-made and were blown complete with smooth lips, with no air bubbles and using much thinner glass. There were no air bubbles in machine-made bottles because the glass was taken out from the bottom of the molten glass and thus there were no bubbles to trap. Old bottles have a seam up the side which stops below the lip (applied afterwards). A.B.M. bottles, the modern type, have a seam running up the side of the bottle *and continuing over the side of the lip.*

The method used for making glass in the 19th century did not produce a colourless glass. This required an additive of a metal oxide to dispel its natural colour. Many common bottles have a greenish tint, known as aqua glass. This colour varied from light green to dark green according to the amount of iron in the sand used in their manufacture. Wood ash and sand were two of the constituents of old bottle glass and both of these produced a variety of green shades.

Old bottles, therefore, could be said to be hand-made one at a time. This gives them individuality and some are a little eccentric with wobbly lips. Whittle marks are "dimples" seen on bottles from wooden moulds, reflecting the uneven surface of the mould on certain types of bottles. By 1920 all bottles were being made automatically and therefore bottles which were literally hand-made or mouth-blown had become obsolete. Secondly, before the metal crimped crown top and the external screw tops were invented, old bottles became the subject of experiments by inventors to find a way of keeping in the gas in fizzy drinks of all kinds. This resulted in the invention of a Mr. Hamilton, patented in 1809 when he brought out a bottle with a pointed base so that the cork—the only stopper available at this time—was always airtight as it was always wet and swollen when laid on its side. Swiss chemist, Jacob Schweppe, set up a chemist's shop in London and was selling the newly-invented artificial fizzy spring water known as aerated water in the early years of the 19th century, and was an early user of the Hamilton bottles to keep in the *schweppervescence.*

Victorian Hamilton bottle from Saffron Walden

However, bottles with a pointed base were difficult to transport and could not be stood upright. Other weird inventions followed. Hiram Codd of London introduced a bottle in 1871 with a rattling glass ball inside which had to be filled upside down and the internal fizzy gas inside the drink pushed the glass ball upwards to seal off the top of the neck. These Codd bottles were often broken by children to extract the glass ball for use as a marble (Victorian marbles were originally made of marble, believe-it-or-not). And I am not talking a load of Codswallop! It is believed this expression, meaning "a load of old rubbish," emanated from the Codd bottles, and if it didn't, it should have. Since then children's marbles have been made of glass. When the glass ball was pushed down to release the gas, the ball dropped into a ridge in the bottle-neck and the release of gas made a "popping" sound. This is believed to be the origin of calling fizzy drinks *pop.*

There were all kinds of inventions for bottle stoppers during the period 1850 to 1910, the most successful for many years was the internal screw-stopper made of vulcanite. Many old codgers of my generation remember these from our childhood. For beer bottles the American invention of the metal crimped crown-top also began to become popular by the 1920s. Invented just after 1900 it was slow to be adopted as it required a special gadget to open it, but it is still popular today for beer bottles. I could continue, but this is not meant to be a book on the history of bottles. I am just pointing out to newcomers the interest to be found in old bottles. And I have not even started on pot-lids! Are old bottles interesting? I would say so. Look them up online on e-bay and buy a book or magazine to get acquainted with what's on offer.

BEAUTIFUL BROWN STONEWARE

Spouted ink bottle and mercury jar

Note the high salt-glaze even after a century of burial

CHAPTER TWO

Finding Town Dumps

It is every dump-digger's dream to find an *un-dug* town dump. They all talk about it. Some do actually dream about it. Yet, though many believe they have all been found and dug out, I know that many dumps must have escaped the digging craze of the 1970s and 80s. Can you seriously believe that 50,000 town rubbish dumps in the U.K. have all been found? Admittedly, some have been built on with trading estates on the outskirts of towns now sitting on top. Admittedly many have been found and badly dug. Admittedly, some have housing estates built on them. Yet I know of two or three large and extremely profitable dumps which have been discovered only in recent years and dug out with a mechanical digger and if you search online you too can watch the digging of one of these on video. I know as a fact that dump-digging still continues in the U.K. but I admit it is more difficult to find somewhere to dig than it was thirty years ago. In these pages I hope to provide clues which will help you to find a dump of some kind which, if you are careful not to publicise it, you can dig out yourself and profit financially from the project and add to your own collection free of charge. You will need to spend some time checking, doing reconnaissance and keep records of where you have been. I cannot guarantee you anything. No-one can. But if you follow my tips, I can promise you will eventually find somewhere to dig up your own relics, your own little treasures. Don't give up too soon. Keep on trying.

Even a small dump in a village can yield finds valued at hundreds of pounds but I do not wish to put too much emphasis on cash values. You can spend a pleasant day out in the country digging up even just a back-pack of antique finds of bewildering variety: glass beers and mineral waters, stoneware ginger beers, salt-glazed polish and blacking pots, ink bottles of many designs, green and cobalt blue poison bottles, beautiful brown-glazed bottles, quack medicine bottles, decorated clay pipe bowls and dolls heads. And there is always the possibility of finding valuable advertising pot-lids, perhaps the odd advertising match-striker and a variety of printed fish paste, jam pots, bone-handled toothbrushes, and many other items. In fact you will find all the detritus of mankind, discarded a century or so ago. Much of it is of relatively low value, but the rarities make it worthwhile. You never know what is going to come up from beneath your feet. I once found a set of Victorian dentures! All the above and many more relics are to be discovered in old dumps.

With the ever-spiralling value of antique bottles and pot-lids and other advertising antiques, an un-dug dump has vastly increased in value in the last twenty years, without anyone knowing of its existence. Whether you dig for profit or for pleasure, or like most of us, a little of both, the finding of an un-dug rubbish dump must be high on your list of priorities. I do not believe anyone digs in dumps just for profit. It is something which provides excitement, and it becomes a drug which cannot be ignored. And if you are new to dump-digging, I envy you. It is an experience once tasted, will never be forgotten. Full-time diggers must always keep on finding new dumps and each year new enthusiasts become hooked. This is why I decided to write this little manual and hopefully it will help most readers to find at least one new digging site.

Why should I be telling you how to find these valuable digging sites? I spent ten years digging mainly in Kent in several towns and later when I moved to live in Westcliffe-on-Sea, Essex, I dug for a while near Dagenham on the banks of the Thames, an old brickworks site now built over. I have also dug in the Wellingborough area and St. Neots once or twice as a guest-digger. I tried my home-town dump at Keighley in Yorkshire, but although the dump there is about forty-feet deep, it has a sports complex on top of it and is lost to this generation. Most of my years were spent on one large brickworks dump on the banks of the Medway in Kent (now out-of-bounds). In spite of rumours, Great Britain is a big country when you search it on foot. I have only traversed a small area of the country. The rest of it I leave to others. Unless you live in the Lake District, the Highlands of Scotland or in Snowdonia, you can bet there is a bottle-site within ten miles of your home. And the world is a big place with the U.K. only a small part of it.

ALLOTMENT GARDENS

Some people chase all over the country digging on recently-opened sites many miles away. One man I knew used to drive to a site sixty miles away every weekend because he couldn't find his own local council dump. When I moved to Sittingbourne in Kent, I found it within a few weeks quite by accident or good luck. I was walking to the large brickworks site one morning and was wearing wellington boots and carried a garden fork under my arm. I said good morning to an old chap digging up plants in his allotment. He seemed curious about my garb and the fork and I stopped for a chat. He told me that he was taking out all his plants from the allotment because he had to quit due to the council planning to build a trading estate on the site. I asked him if he had ever dug up any clay pipes or old bits of blue or green glass and he told me he did. I told him I was interested in finding old bottles and he then invited me to dig at the bottom of his allotment which he had already cleared of plants. About two-feet down I hit a layer of town refuse and that very day I found the first local pot-lid found in Sittingbourne at that time. It was a toothpaste lid from a local High Street chemist, Mr. Gordelier, depicting the local church only a few hundred yards away from the site. I was curious as to why the chemist chose to depict a church on his toothpaste and found out from the vicar that Mr. Gordelier, the chemist, used to be the church organist around 1910. This lid was probably valued at about £30 to £40 at the time, (I believe I sold it to that famous Texan collector, Colonel Ben Swanson who lived in the U.K. then and visited me weekly to check my new finds) but as a piece of valuable local history and an attractive and rare lid, I could see it today selling today for around £200 or possibly more to a keen collector. I only know of one other example found there. This dump yielded several more pot-lids, but all from national companies and being a provincial town, the number of lids found in it were far less than from the richer London refuse of the brickworks. There's rubbish and better rubbish! The lesson: talk to people about your hobby. But don't talk to other bottle-diggers about where you dig. I made the mistake of selling some of the local Sittingbourne ginger-beers and mineral water bottles in my auctions after I found the local dump. Big mistake! The local lads were up in arms at a Yorkshireman coming into their home town and finding the local dump when they couldn't find it. One of them followed me from my home one morning and the secret was out. Within a week I was digging with eight other people alongside me. We dug there even when the bulldozers came in to build the trading estate. We waited for them finishing work about 4 p.m. and worked there until dark. When you find a new site and it's a local dump with the town named on your finds, it's advisable to keep all your finds until you have cleared out the dump. Then you can sell them!

I must emphasise that there is no magic formula for finding dumps. It requires research and a lot of persistence. Although I had a massive brickworks dump on my doorstep for ten years, every now and then I fancied a change and with my digging partner (it is always safer to dig with a trusted friend) we used to pick a town we had never been to before and take a train. If you have a car it is convenient, but do not park your car at the roadside where you are digging. It is a dead give-away that someone is lurking around in the woods or wherever you are digging. This can attract unwelcome attention and other diggers. On a reconnaissance trip such as we did now and then, it pays to get out of your car and walk! It also requires know-how. I can give you that know-how and the research and persistence is down to you. By the time you have finished reading this manual you will probably already have a few ideas where you might try searching.

I did most of my digging with just an ordinary garden fork because the brickworks dumps were pretty solid with bricks and half-bricks mixed in. It would be impossible to dig on such a site with a spade or shovel. However, if you do travel by car, by all means take a spade or shovel with you for these normal sites contain much loose soil. Use the fork for digging as spades do more damage to the finds. In summer I always wore army-type boots with a strong toe-cap, but in winter when you could be standing in water, wellington boots are the dress of the day. But be careful not to allow refuse to cover your boots when digging. It's so easy to put a fork through your tootsies. Believe me, it hurts!

Victorian pot-lid for an ointment to cure all problems

A practical plan to find yourself a council dump is to choose a small town or large village (very small villages may not have their own dump) which is not too far away from your home and concentrate on this. It is far more satisfying to find your own dump and dig it with a friend than to dig shoulder to shoulder with the "mob" on these very large dumps which become invaded by people from all over the country. Buy a good map of the area and pinpoint possible dump sites on it before you leave home.

THE FIRST PLACE TO LOOK

You could find a dump within a few hours of arriving in the town or village you have chosen. It could take two or three trips. Don't give up after one failed attempt. Before you go, check on an Ordnance Survey map to find where the Sewage Works and Gas Works are or were. Tip no.1: the smelly businesses were always located on the edges of a town. You will often find the Gas Works, Sewage Works and Rubbish Dump are all near each other. This is not always the case, but it is the first place to look. You are looking for a piece of land possibly raised up above the level of surrounding land. It will probably have nettles, brambles and elderberry bushes growing on it (a sign of disturbed land). It might not be raised up, but often is. If flat and covered with nettles, it could still be a dump. However, it might just be an industrial dump, full of old stones and rusty cans, but you will only find out by digging into it. I realise that many gasworks have now disappeared from our landscapes but when they were in use, one of the giant gas-holders containing gas floated on water, pushed up from water in the other tank which was full of water on a kind of see-saw basis. When gas levels rose up in one, water in the other tank went down. For this process to work gasworks were usually built as near to rivers as possible. Similarly, sewage works need the proximity of a river to function. Find these two places and this is where you should begin your search for a nearby dump. I have stated "start" your search deliberately as there is no hard-and-fast rule. I can only state that the three smelly operations were *usually* sited near each other, for obvious reasons on the outskirts of town and near a river or creek. Check all round the area of the sewage works and gasworks sites thoroughly. Any suspect piece of land should be test-dug before trying elsewhere. And don't just poke about one foot below the surface. Remember, council dumps were often covered over with clay or rubble to seal them as a deterrent against smells and vermin. You need to dig down at least three feet on a test dig.

As I have explained, I spent most of my digging years on brickworks dumps which contained only London refuse taken into Kent on barges up the Thames and Medway rivers and taken off the barges to be dumped on the riverside brickworks fields. All the bottles and pot-lids had no local names on them, always coming from large national companies. Although London refuse contained far more pot-lids than local council dumps because there were more affluent residents in the capital, local dumps are far more interesting, with names of local companies on them, as do the pot-lids. A pot-lid from a local chemist has a local history interest and additionally there are not many of them in existence. Check the prices of the Woods 6d tooth-paste and Burgess's Anchovy Paste pot-lids (just a few pounds), the two most commonly-found lids sold throughout the country. There are many thousands of them around, but not many of Joe Bloggs, High Street chemist of Little Diddley, Hertfordshire, for example. It can, therefore, be seen that local town council dumps are the ones to search for. (Woods pots or bases have an impressed "W" underneath and Burgess's pots have the no. "30" impressed and are therefore easy to match up with their lids)

I would advise you to forget the big towns and cities as these large dumps may well have been found and dug by the frenzied mass diggings which took place in the 70s and 80s, being more easily found. I remember once allowing myself to be taken to dig at a large dump near Bedford many years ago and the place was a mess. Random digging was taking place with holes everywhere, soil thrown out onto un-dug areas and about 60 people all getting into everyone else's way. The site resembled a First World War battlefield with shell-craters everywhere. I made some finds, but it was not pleasurable by any means. I never returned.

SMALL WOODED AREAS

If you don't find your dump in your target town or village in the vicinity of its sewage works and gas works, there are other places you can try. As an example, my digging partner and I once decided to visit a certain small Kent seaside town. We had never been there before, but we could not find the dump near the gasworks as it had housing all around it. In desperation we used the F.O.M. method—*Find an Old Man*. Old men are usually those with wrinkly faces and bent shoulders. They are often supported with a wooden stick, and though apt to hibernate in winter, they are more prevalent in summer. They can often be seen on park benches in memorial gardens in bunches, cowering in corners of local hostelries or pottering about in their gardens, pretending to work. They can usually speak without too much difficulty when accosted, but most respond to a pint of throat-oil which lubricates and loosens the tongue. For the price of a beer, if they are a native of the area, they can remember where the rubbish was dumped when they were young as in the old days, rubbish dumps were not enclosed and young boys spent many happy hours there. If he is not a local, you can always ask him where the dump was in his own native town, wherever it was. Of course, in the 21st century you are not going to encounter any old man who remembers an Edwardian dump, most likely it would be 1940's, but this could lead you to a much earlier dump underneath it or alongside it.

In this particular case, the old man in his garden told us, "You'll never find it." We told him we hadn't. He told us to walk up the main road a few hundred yards and to turn left on to a dirt track. "Follow that track a couple of hundred yards," he said, "and you'll come across a small wood on the left. That's the dump." Walking down the dirt track the sun highlighted glints of broken coloured glass beneath our feet: brown Bovril glass and cobalt blue and green poison bottle fragments. We knew then he wasn't lying. The trees in the small wood were about 50yrs.old, I guessed. (Learning to roughly date trees is a good idea for bottle-diggers) A couple of trees were actually growing through old tin bath-tubs, so it was obvious the dump was not sealed in with clay or soil. The moment we sank our forks into the ground, bright green mineral water bottles began popping up, all bright and clean as a whistle. This was in the 1970s and the finds were 1920s, confirming the age of the trees. The lack of pot-lids was compensated by the fact that most bottles were "takers," not being burnt red with ashes or "sick" from being underwater as is often encountered on riverside brickworks sites. This had obviously been a pit or depression filled in, providing good drainage. There were many Codd bottles and printed ginger-beers (not salt-glazed as in earlier dumps). Another benefit was the finding of two or three very large German bisque dolls heads complete with swivel-eyes. But one thing bugged us: there didn't seem to be enough material there. We dug this out in less than a week, by visiting it every day. Once opened up, it was imperative not to hang about before others also found the exposed material. It was just a shallow layer about three to four feet deep, which had been dumped and left for nature to cover it with weeds, bushes and trees. After we had finished this dump we had a good walkabout around the outskirts of town after checking small woods on our map. This is imperative. You may need the car to move about but you need to park it somewhere unobtrusive and do some walking. Scan the area, looking for raised mounds of land. These shout at you. Others don't. O.K., there are none of these. On dirt tracks leading off a tarmac road, check for signs of old glass and pottery. Check small roadside woods. Cross each one off as you check them as some small woods will be just small woods, or may contain a spring or remains of old farm buildings. Some, we found, contained refuse.

Check woods in ploughed land if you are not causing damage to land and crops. In this town we noticed a golf course in the distance, just outside town and by poking around in all small woods nearby, we found two more dumps during that week, both of small size, but slightly earlier than the first, probably from about 1910 to 1920, containing a few pot-lids. Golf courses are another place to search (the outskirts, not the course) if not found by the two smelly places. Another area to search is near rifle-ranges and on river banks. Before you set out for a new town, check the map and sort out these areas which seem most likely before you even leave home. Look for the areas where the following places are located, usually on the edges of town, and often near a river. Gasworks, sewage works, golf courses, rifle ranges, river banks, allotments, are all likely places to search. This way you know before you arrive at a village the areas on your map you are going to search. One more tip: during World War Two most towns and even small villages turned spare plots of land into allotment gardens so that people could help the war effort by growing their own vegetables. Many of these are still in use, but many have since been abandoned. Some of these were created on top of old dumps. Have a chat with allotment holders. Ask if they have seen signs of clay pipe stems and broken glass or pottery. Talk to the locals in pubs or those old men lurking about. Ask questions. Are there any abandoned allotments around? It may turn out that the local dump has already been found and dug, but until you know this for certain, you continue searching. If you still can't find the dump or if you are told it has already been dug, then you can move on to your next target town. But not before checking the old dug site if there is one. (More about re-digging old dug sites in a later chapter)

In another village not far away from the first one, we once spotted a circle of 50 year-old trees in the middle of a ploughed field. By a bit of surreptitious creeping alongside a wall, we reached it without being seen and again it was a 1920s dump: we suspected this by asking, "Why would a farmer allow trees to grow in the middle of a ploughed field?" Farmers are not normally wasteful. We found three such digging sites like this all around this small Kent town. If the trees had been a century old (in 1975) we would not have had to check it, but the age of the trees was a clue.

In our search for dumps we are definitely going to encounter more modern dumps from the 1920s to the 1940s, say. Whilst the bottles from these types of dump will not be mouth-blown with hand-applied lips as in pre-1914 dumps, they can still be worth digging, but read about these later.

You have targeted one town. You have gone there and checked all possible areas pre-determined as I advised. You have talked to old men. You have not found that there was a dump which was dug out thirty years ago. O.K. Where do you go from here? Either the village was too small to have its own dump and its refuse was taken to the nearest larger town's dump or it is in some unlikely spot. If you have genuinely checked the area as advised within these pages and you really cannot find the dump, there is only one conclusion. It has been built over. I can give you an example of this from my own village. I moved into my present home in Hertfordshire when I retired 15 years ago. It is a village of about 2,300 population today, with about half that in 1900. I soon found out where the gasworks used to be but found the site was now covered over by a new estate of riverside houses. (Note what I said about rivers and gasworks) I eventually became acquainted with someone who lived in one of these houses. This person told me that in their garden they found bits of old glass and pottery and I was invited to look. There was only a narrow strip of soil around the lawn, but poking about between the plants I found pieces of clay pipes and old bottle glass of various colours. Enquiries from old men lurking outside the local inn confirmed that the rubbish dump and gasworks had indeed once been down the riverside until the new estate was built. When this happens, you have to either give up or buy a house! If all else fails you just have to get out your map and pick anther target town or village. You may feel you have wasted your time on one or two visits, but most such exploration can be achieved in one day. You will feel disappointed, but it is not all negative. You have had a healthy walk and possibly gained some experience. And you have become acquainted with a town you have never been to before. Just cross that village off your list of targets and move on to the next. If you work, you can have one pleasant day out in the fresh air once a week until you find your dump.

Not all towns had a council dump in 1900, especially small villages. If you do find a dump in a small village, it is unlikely to have had a dump so early. You just have to be satisfied with a later dump if that is the case. A couple of examples: a town of 50,000 inhabitants today began dumping about 1895. Another of about 15,000 inhabitants today began dumping about 1910. One other factor to consider: if you do find a dump dating from the 1920s (with no pot-lids but with transfer printed stoneware ginger beers), it may have an earlier section. This could either be underneath the later material, so you must ensure that you don't just dig the top three or four feet and leave the more valuable, earlier material beneath it. Dig to the very bottom of the dump, the clay bed, before abandoning it. On the other hand, if the dump is shallow, say about three feet, the other end of the dump may have been started first, ten or more years earlier. To sum up, one way or another you must dig your dump to its extreme. Otherwise you will be leaving the best behind. (See section on efficient digging later)

In the coastal resort previously mentioned, the refuse was not in one big dump as would be expected, but scattered about in various places, possibly infilling hollows, which had eventually become small woods over the intervening years. One other accidental find was given to me by a relative who was a soldier in the Royal Engineers, based at Chattenden Barracks, Kent. Whilst on a five-mile-bash with the army, he had seen similar old bottles to those in my shop, way out in the countryside. He said the rabbits had dug them up whilst burrowing. Being a soldier he was able to pinpoint exactly where the area was on my map, and we went out there to investigate. It was about half-a-mile from the road. There was a stream or ditch, dug exactly in a straight line (militarily) a few yards outside a dense wood. When first dug, the soil from this ditch had been thrown up on one side and this was where the bottles were peeping out by rabbit burrowing. The entire length of the ditch was about two hundred yards and, being very shallow, about two feet, we dug the mound between us in one day. It was the strangest digging-site I can remember. No pot-lids, no medicines or cures, simply glass beer and mineral water bottles with a few clay pipes. Most of the bottles were the attractive green Magnum pop bottles of Hills Chapman with the heavy embossing, and as all collectors know, they are all dated on the base. These ranged from 1908 to 1918. Have you already guessed? I later discovered that before and during the First World War, soldiers had their Lines here (lines of tents that is). A military dump made by soldiers and found by a soldier more than 60 years later. The ditch had probably been dug by soldiers to drain the land for their tenting. The Magnum bottles, although attractive, were not very welcome at the time, being very common, but I wouldn't mind finding about sixty of them today inside a few hours as they were in perfect condition.

As was our custom, we returned to the area next day after recovering from our strenuous efforts taking such a heavy load back to the car. We walked for over an hour in the vicinity and the only thing we found was a gigantic mound, which was obviously refuse of some kind, but was only 100 yards away from the farmhouse. We were on a public footpath and we tossed a coin to see who was going to knock on the farm door. I lost. I explained to the farmer's wife that we were bottle collectors, interested in local history, blah, blah, blah, and she more or less told us to clear off her private property as if her husband returned he would turn his shotgun on us and she wouldn't be responsible and he could finish up on a murder charge as he didn't like strangers on his land and he had a quick temper. I guessed she was saying "no" and discreetly retraced my steps. To be fair, if a stranger knocked on my door with a garden fork in his hand and asked to dig into a pile of rubbish at the bottom of my garden, I would probably be suspicious too. Sometimes our obsession with finding relics overtakes our discretion, as others do not always share our enthusiasm.

Another small dump I was invited to was near St. Neots, with the owner's permission, provided we left his pheasants alone. I went there by train from London. The main part of the dump was in a very smelly hollow *in a small wood.* The bottles were alongside this swamp and also in it. Rubbish from the estate had obviously been dumped in a pond which had now become a very smelly quagmire. We had not gone prepared for this and we were both wearing ordinary boots. Eventually we had to take our boots and socks off and dig in the thick mud. I would not normally have done so, but the finds were so good. It was a real red letter day. Along the banks of this thick black smelly mud wild garlic grew, adding an unusual aroma to the already offensive smell. Soon we took our shirts off as we had to feel around under the mud up to our elbows to extract the bottles. We were up to our knees in the stuff eventually and reeking of putrefaction from the mud. It was here in this goo that I retrieved over 20 bullet-stopper bottles and where I found a whole rusty dustbin which contained five complete Warner's Safe Cure bottles and four pot-lids, all within minutes. At that time a Warner's bottle (one-pint green) was fetching £15 and I went home that day with about £150 of "goodies." I cannot remember the name of the friend who invited me to dig there, but I do remember that I gave him one of my Warner's bottles as a thank-you.

I did my best to remove the mud from myself afterwards with no access to water, but had to wait until I was on the train to wash myself over in the toilet. Even when cleaned up a bit, I was sitting down next to nice clean people who were looking askance at my muddy clothing and sniffing audibly, wondering why I smelled of garlic. If you were one of those people on the train that day, turning your nose up at me, you had probably only earned a fraction of what I had in my bag, so there! The pheasant had a nice garlic flavour too.

One lesson to be learned from all these occasions is that small woods are always worth checking, providing you are not trespassing on private land as some farmers can be quite aggressive. Having said that, one or two farmers I have approached have been very interested in the bottles on their land and have been happy to give permission to dig after giving them one or two bottles and explain their history. And I was only joking about the pheasant!

Edwardian French mustard jar

CHAPTER THREE

Brickworks Dumps

I have already explained that from about 1850, brickworks brought London refuse back on the old spritsail or Thames and Medway barges as they are called. Some of these old red-sailed barges have survived and are brought out for an annual river festival. Those of the brickworks were used in the 19th century and up to about the 1940s to deliver their bricks to London and instead of coming back empty, they filled up with the "rough stuff," unsorted London refuse. This was dumped on the brickworks land and the fine ash sieved from it. This was then added to the pug clay to make fine London bricks. The remainder of the refuse had a degree of combustibility as it contained small pieces of half-burnt coal, wood and other household waste and it was used as fuel in a kiln to bake the bricks. This "rough stuff" was sorted into three categories by sieving: *Soil* is the very fine gritty ash used to mix with clay to make bricks. *Breeze* is small pieces of coke, clinker and cinders. This is the combustible content used in the kiln. Finally, *Core* is the hardcore—the bottles, stoneware, pot-lids, dolls heads—all the material we want. The kiln was made outside by creating a layer of bricks, topped with a layer of breeze, another layer of bricks and another layer of breeze and so on. Then the whole was covered with a mountain of hardcore for insulation. When fired, the breeze burnt slowly to carry heat throughout the kiln. It is for this reason that many valuable glass bottles were melted and when digging in this material, many finds were not in good enough condition to keep. Bottles in distorted shapes with an iridescent colour came out of these burnt areas of the brickworks kilns. Earthenware was ruined similarly and some pot-lids survived with red burn patches. If you see a cherry toothpaste lid advertised on e-bay with red marks on it, don't believe the vendor if he tells you it's cherry toothpaste which is discolouring the lid. It's a burn mark and is impossible to remove. Cherry-coloured toothpaste *would* be removable.

The hardcore was not needed by the brickworks after firing and was just dumped on their land away from the buildings and working areas after being used to surround the kiln. The material closest to the heat was obviously damaged, but the outside material was not and this is the material in which we made our finds. This is why the brickworks people tolerated diggers helping themselves to the hardcore for many years. It was of no use to them. Mass invasions from all over Britain and accidents to diggers on their land finally caused them to close the site down and to build on it.

I have talked to many old retired "brickies" who worked at the brickworks in the 1930s and 40s. One old man told me that they used to find many perks in the "rough stuff" when he was a sorter and on one occasion he found some gold sovereigns in an old mattress which came off the barges. They also found useful bike frames, and sometimes coins down the seats of old chairs and settees. Once they found a dead donkey and they buried it with the men taking off their hats and one saying some suitable donkey words.

I have to admit that I just don't know how brickworks operated in the rest of the country. I do know that for ten years I lived within a stone's throw of the biggest brickworks dump in the U.K. It is now out of bounds to all. It lasted 10years for me and I actually moved there to live near it. When I lived in Sittingbourne I remember a coach pulling up outside my house one Saturday. It had come from Glasgow and was occupied by about 30 Scottish bottle-diggers. I was writing much in those days for *Treasure Hunting* magazine when it used to include dump-digging in its pages. One chap knocked on my door and asked, "Are you Ron Dale, the bottle man?" I could not deny it. "We've come down to dig on your dump. Can you tell us where it is?" I could not refuse a coach-load of Scots who had travelled all that way. I went to the dump with them and it was so vast that it had poor areas, medium areas and special areas. I took them to the medium areas and left them to their own devices.

Dozens of brickworks existed in the 19th and early 20th century, far more than today. Many have closed down. Not all brickworks used dustbin ash to make bricks. Some used sand to mix with the clay, so some local research is necessary here. If dustbin ash was used in your local brickworks, start digging.

On the Thames and Medway the sailing barges needed no fuel and were a very economical form of transport. I believe other parts of the country did have some brickworks alongside rivers, creeks and canals, but I honestly don't know if they used refuse for the coal ash content. Some of these old brickworks, even if now abandoned, may still be around if not built over. This will need research at local level, *paying particular attention to those sited near rivers, creeks or canals.*

Due to the history of London refuse being bought on the river for use in the brickworks before refuse was commercially dumped, the earliest dump I have dug of this London rough stuff was 1850s. Just in one patch on the brickworks did I ever find anything so early. It was here I discovered a small plant-pot shaped blacking pot as described by Charles Dickens when he worked for his uncle at Warren's Blacking factory in London. In one of his books he describes how as a young boy he put a waxed paper top over these pots and tied string around them. It is not much to look at: just a small salt-glazed plant pot about four inches high, but the Dickens connection intrigued me. Later blacking bottles were cylindrical, of course and larger. It was here I found a clay pipe bowl with the Crystal Palace building displayed on the sides of the bowl, with "Pipes for All Nations" advertising on it from the 1851 Exhibition in Hyde Park. It was here also that I was near to tears as I slowly and carefully teased out what I thought was a very early blue printed bear's grease lid, but it turned out to be only about 60% of a lid. Most of the other material was from about 1870 to 1910. The brickworks was also the only dump where I regularly dug what I called "submarine" poison bottles with the word "poison" embossed alongside the rugby ball shape of the bottle. I have never found these in any other dump and had to presume they were reasonably early, probably 1870 to 1880.

As far as I am concerned, there are no brickworks digging sites accessible today in the areas I have mentioned and I would not wish to mislead anyone. However, forever optimistic, there is no harm in doing a little local research on brickworks in your own locality and how they operated. Did they use refuse? If so, is the land still accessible? The digging on my brickworks was a phenomenon. It was something none of us appreciated at the time and we thought it could last forever. Dozens of part-time diggers went there every weekend and for me it was my daily place of work. Nothing lasts forever. For this reason we must ensure that we always empty a dump completely. You never know where your next one is coming from.

Giant-sized Christmas pipe for communal smoking in a pub

CHAPTER FOUR

Other Types of Dump

Antique refuse is all around us. And it is not always in heaped-up mounds as this would not be a complete picture of the disposal of refuse. I have already pointed out that refuse can be scattered about in fields to fill in hollows which have now become small areas of woodland in ploughed fields. Knowing what happened to the rubbish of bye-gone days would be an aid to finding it, and although it may be widely dispersed, it still exists for us to find.

From about 1835 to 1850 as already explained, London's refuse was sold off to use in Essex, Sussex, Kent and other counties for land reclamation, in addition for use in brickworks. Obviously for land reclamation, we are talking about coastal areas and anyone who has been involved in diving or in dredging operations in harbours will tell you that there are thousands of antique bottles in the sea. I am not suggesting we should all go diving for bottles, but I am saying that such finds in coastal areas may point to refuse washed out of land nearby..

These coastal fields will not show any outward signs of containing very early London refuse—the period 1835-1850 would be a valuable period for finds. Farmers are more likely to find signs of refuse when ploughing, so some communication here is necessary. If you spot sign of broken coloured glass in a ploughed field, have a word with the farmer.

Roads and railways were often shored up with refuse. I have mentioned one road I know of in Northamptonshire which was dug for a short time.

I am not advocating we dig up roads and railways, but often roads are dug up or widened by local councils. And sometimes rail lines are closed down or have been already closed down for many years.

It is important for diggers to keep abreast of what is happening in their own area regarding new motorways or major road-works etc. as I have found that bulldozer drivers are always happy to earn a few pounds extra by doing an extra half-hour after working hours or in picking up pot-lids during the day if spotted!

PRIVATE HOUSE DUMPS

I have saved the best for last. I believe these types of dumps offer today's diggers the most possibilities for digging. Large country houses, farms, mansions and manor houses would have had no collection of their refuse in the 19th century. With the exception of London, refuse collection did not begin in large cities until about 1880. Smaller towns may have started collections from about 1895 onwards and dates for this vary greatly. Large country houses or even smaller houses and farms in rural areas probably did not have collections until after 1900 and in some areas much later. I have to state "may have" or "could have" as it is difficult to be more precise; every council made individual arrangements. This being the case, we can take it for granted that isolated country houses could not have had any collection throughout the whole of the 19th century and if in some areas they did, it would have only been for the last few years of the century. The period of production of transfer-printed pot-lids is roughly from about the 1840s up to ro the 1914-18 period. Some large companies such as Atkinson's and the polychrome Pegwell Bay series were continued as a prestige gimmick for nostalgic reasons into the 1920s.

The implication here is obvious. What happened to their refuse throughout all those Victorian years? This is the period of pot-lids, the period of valuable quack bottles and of Hamiltons and Codds and all those early stopper inventions and the period of beautiful cobalt blue poison bottles. And it is the period of hybrids, where two inventions were tried in one bottle, such as the Codd-Hamilton hybrid. It is the period we would all like to dig in, surely. A dump of this type could contain collectables valued at £20,000 plus.

Only last week I was doing some research on such a large manor house in another part of the county with the co-operation of the owners and discovered that in 1881 the owners held a huge party in their grounds for about 400 people and I came across reports in a local newspaper that the visitors were treated to tables creaking with large joints of beef and lamb. And *"2,000 bottles of ginger beer, practically all of which were consumed."*

Unfortunately for the modern collector, the 2,000 bottles dumped in one day would have been plain salt-glazed bottles as transfer printed ginger beers were not in use then, but even so, that's a lot of bottles to be found. Add to these all the bottles and pot-lids the wealthy family would have used since it was built earlier in the century and we are talking about a very valuable dump. The assumption must be that all these collectables are still there, somewhere. All country houses and farms with land attached would naturally have dumped their rubbish on their own land. And in most cases it is still there!

The ginger beer bottles on their own would not be very valuable, assuming that half of them are still intact, but they do have some value. Wealthy families would certainly have used toothpaste, cold cream, medicinal ointment, bear's grease, shaving cream, lip salve, etc. and on their property could be over 50 years of their pot-lids. Imagine a dump dating from 1840 to 1900 untouched! The pot-lids alone could be worth many thousands of pounds. Now how many large country houses would you consider exist in Great Britain which were occupied throughout the Victorian period. I live in a small village and I know of ten such houses. Some of these have become country hotels. Multiply this by about 50,000 (the number of towns and villages listed in a 1904 Gazetteer) and this comes to 500,000 houses. Half a million houses with a hidden Victorian dump once owned by people who were wealthy or at least not poor! What treasure there must be lurking in the woods nearby or buried in some pit or in a pond, down a well, or where? That is the burning question. And don't forget, country mansions are not the only houses surviving from previous centuries. Many farms were also built prior to say, 1880, and were also likely to have their own private dumping ground.

If the house is a period house dating from the 16th, 17th or 18th century, there is also the possibility of finding really valuable seal bottles. The onion-shaped bottles of the 17th century gradually gave way to the mallet-shaped ones of the 18th century, when it was discovered that corks do not dry out if you lay the wine bottle down on its side so that the wine soaks the cork and makes it airtight. Onion-shaped bottles could only stand upright. This caused the production of cylindrical bottles of dumpy shape which could be laid down on their sides. The heavy tax on glass made wine bottles expensive which only the wealthy could afford. It was not until 1845 that wine was sold by the bottle in this country. Prior to that date wealthy people had their own bottles made, often bearing a glass disc, known as a seal, because it often portrayed their seal, coat of arms or initials, for identification. These seal bottles were sent to the wine merchant for filling from the barrel and the "seal" identified the name of the owner. As most bottle collectors know these seal bottles, especially if the owners are traceable and if also dated, can be worth several thousand pounds each. Even such early bottles without a seal have some value, but nowhere near the sealed type. The fact that these family seals were used is a point to mention to your country house owner (if the house is old enough) as he would be very interested I feel sure, to possess a bottle owned by his ancestor with the family crest or initials on it. Don't forget to point this out as it could make all the difference to gaining permission to dig. You may be content with your share of Victorian finds. Many years ago I remember a manor house in Ubley, Avon, where a 17th century sealed wine bottle was found under the floorboards when renovations were being done. Four such bottles were found together embedded in soil at the entrance to an earthed-up cellar with the initials "IAL" (I meaning J in this century) and the owner was traced to a member of the Loupe family, dated from circa 1670, and was subsequently sold at Sotheby's auction in November, 1982. Unfortunately I do not have a record of the price, but today it would be

£1000s. In 1976 two Shropshire farm-workers, Bob Pell and Ron Warden were digging a rather exhausted Victorian dump for bottles and pot-lids *in a wood, on the banks of a river.* Suddenly they discovered a complete onion-shaped bottle of circa 1700 in date, whilst digging on the perimeter of the Victorian dump. They then did some research and discovered the area was once the site of a medieval castle which had been demolished to make way for a grand mansion house, which had also since been demolished. By checking engravings of the mansion, it was found that a tunnel had been constructed from the kitchen to the riverside, probably solely for the dumping of household waste. They then concentrated their digging on the land around the exit of the tunnel, where they unearthed several more early onion bottles and clay pipes of the17th & 18th century. This is an example of a combination of luck and research. But what if they had done the research first? Have you any old mansions or medieval properties which were demolished in your area? Keep your eyes and ears open for these. And can you research them online or in your local library?

Right and left, mallet-shaped bottles (18th cent.)
Centre, onion-shape (17th cent.)

One way or another, such private house dumps are probably the most interesting and most valuable any treasure-seeker can find. Ordinary dustbin relics from a town dump were discarded by mostly poor people with some middle-class and a just a few rich people. Private house dumps of the calibre we are discussing were all owned by wealthy families. They could afford luxury items which the general populace could not. A labouring man in 1870, for example, would not buy a pot of toothpaste costing 6d. If he cleaned his teeth at all, he would use salt. The preponderance of pot-lids in private house dumps is much higher than in town refuse. *Occupants of these houses are more likely to have used the rare bottles we all covet. They are more likely to have used bears grease and the more expensive commodities such as those contained in submarine poison bottles and the many quack cures which working-class people could not afford.* Add to this, the possibility in older houses of finding seal bottles of the 17th and 18th century, and this makes these dumps even more desirable to dump diggers, being a double bonus. I think I have made my point strongly enough here.

Having said all this, such dumps are not the easiest to find. One modern benefit not often used today for dump-finding is the internet. If you make a list of potential country houses to investigate, you can have a look around them without leaving home by using Google Earth. With this facility you can have a look around the area without leaving home. You will obviously not spot a dump from this, but you *might* spot potential areas to start looking.

The owners of these country house dumps are not likely to know of the existence and value of early refuse on his land. He may settle for a lump sum, provided you are sure of some return by doing a test dig. What kind of agreement you make with the owner is up to you, but there are several ways to achieve this. The main problem is first to locate the area where refuse was dumped over a century ago and this is not always easy. Farm records if they exist can be helpful. All waste land is suspect, especially in small woods. Even ploughed fields may have had hollows filled in and covered with soil to make the field completely ploughable. Traces of broken glass and clay pipe fragments are always a clue here. Forget 50 yr. old trees on these sites. We are looking for a dump site dating from about 1850 to 1900 with the optimistic possibility of the added bonus of finds from an earlier date, depending on the age of the property.

It is possible that the Victorian refuse has been grassed over to make a lawn. Large lawns can hide a multitude of bins. It may have been built over by garages and other outbuildings. But in 99% of cases, I estimate that the refuse from the 19th century and even from the 18th and 17th century is still there somewhere. And don't forget ponds. These can be drained or dredged. And many ponds are several centuries old. Who knows what lurks in their bottom mud. And if there is farmland attached to the house, talk to the farm-hands who plough the land.

The search for a dump on a period country house will not always be successful. Some owners of country houses are just not interested in finding them. (Mention the possible value of £20,000 to £30,000 and they will not believe you) This is an unfortunate fact we have to face. But if one is found you can be assured of valuable finds—more valuable than in any dump you have ever dug. And you do not have to declare it to the coroner or any government department. The treasure is all yours and the land-owner's if this is your agreement. If you do manage to make a contract or verbal agreement with the owner of a country mansion, it would be advisable to make a contract which is legally binding with both parties sharing equally the finds or the cash value of the finds when sold. Metal detectorists have these contract forms, so try to obtain one and copy it. Also ask the house owner if he has any old plans of the property from the 19th century so that you know exactly where the kitchen used to be then and check for ponds in the grounds which may or may not still exist. Often ponds were filled in with rubbish and if still a wet area, sometimes the outline of the pond can be spotted by the shape of waterside reeds still growing today. Existing ponds would need to be dredged in some way. A rowing boat on a large pond with a home-made dredging device could be useful here. Ancient ponds often contain ancient relics, coins, etc.

Starting at the kitchen door, stand there and consider. Where would they dump rubbish? Is there a stream nearby or a ditch? Was there a nearby pond? Is there or was there a quarry nearby. No-one would wish to move heavy smelly refuse too far, and certainly not uphill. One tip: if you find the Victorian dump, it is highly likely that the earlier dump is nearby. People are creatures of habit and if a site is ideal to dump rubbish on in the 17th and 18th century, the chances are that this would continue in the 19th century. So we come back to looking for Victorian refuse again. Pieces of clay pipes date the material for us. Decorated bowls with the bowl at an angle of about 90 degrees to the stem are late Victorian, with the earlier centuries with plain bowls being much smaller and at a much larger angle to the stem. Ask your house-owner if he or any of the family have encountered signs of broken glass, pottery and clay pipes. And if you do find the Victorian dump, ensure you dig down to solid clay and beyond its perimeter to find the earlier, valuable seal bottles. You are looking for material in a hole deeper than the surrounding clay. For example, let's assume the refuse was dumped in a hollow to fill it up to the level of surrounding land and you have already dug a test hole to find clay at three-feet. This is where a probing rod of six or more feet long will come in handy. The pointed rod will find clay at three feet. If it suddenly disappears to four or five feet, you know a hollow has been filled in and you will dig there. It all sounds a bit hit-and-miss and it is, but trial and error is the only way. Of course all this research may not be necessary. Sometimes the house-owner knows already where the old rubbish was dumped but does not know it has a value. Here you might be on sticky ground as, after you telling him it is valuable, he might just show you off his property and dig it himself!

Finding a private house dump involves as much research as possible by you and the owner plus a large amount of common-sense, hard work and an element of luck. Sometimes out-buildings may cover up your dump or even a large lawn and if this is the case you are out of luck. Personally, I would sacrifice a fine lawn for an un-dug bottle dump any day, but not everyone is as enthusiastic. Sometimes you just cannot win, but the rewards are high and worth a try. You may have to do a lot of test holes. And please remember, in olden days people were less hygiene-conscious than we are today. We would not dump household waste anywhere near our house, but they may not have been so fussy in the 18th or 19th centuries.

One example of my own experience was at an 18th century farmhouse in Kent, where I was actually asked to look for a dump by the owner who was interested in antique bottles. I naturally started at his kitchen door and soon spotted a clump of nettles in a small paddock about twenty-five yards from his kitchen door. The nettles were growing on a small mound, only a few yards in circumference against a stone wall. A close look showed pieces of broken coloured glass, pieces of pottery and a couple of the rough-shaped aqua glass "marbles" from Codd bottles: all the signs of an Edwardian or turn-of-the-century dump. Unfortunately, the owner turned the tables on me and said he didn't want to dig it just yet. He just wanted me to find it. He did make a nice cup of tea and salmon and cucumber sandwiches, but I would rather have had a dig in his nettles. He later told me that the site was the top of an old well he was unaware of until he dug it out.

If you do dig in the grounds of an ancient or even a Victorian manor house, you are going to have to do some very serious digging if you wish to dig back two centuries or more. If you are sure of the existence of a dump, a mechanical digger can be hired or borrowed if it is worth the expense. A metal detector on a Victorian dump would be buzzing all the time and would be unsuitable, but if you find an 18th or 17th century site, coins and artefacts from this date would be of value and here a metal detector could be useful.

It is obvious that every country house would present an individual problem to solve and I cannot tell you where to look. However, there are certain tips I can give you to help you make a start looking. But first you will need to engage the interest of the present owner, most of them being at least reasonably affluent! So would they be interested in you offering them a share in the profits or a share in a load of old bottles? If approached discreetly first, possibly by letter, pointing out that you are a bottle collector, interested in local history and a member of the Diggemup Bottle Club (or whatever) and that you would like to investigate on their land with a view to finding collectable Victorian rubbish. You are, of course, willing to share the spoils with them on a 50-50 basis, as do treasure hunters with metal detectors. They may refuse point blank or ignore your letter. A polite phone call if ignored might enable you to close this down as a refusal. There are plenty more. Some house-owners, especially the younger generation, become interested and if so, show them some early bottles and pot-lids from your collection to get them interested. Those who run the house as a bed and breakfast house or country hotel are more likely to be interested as they are in business to make money and most businesses are suffering. They might even wish to participate. In my experience about one in three become interested and this is often the younger generation of the family between. It is the older generation who cannot be bothered to have strangers on their property.

Let us assume that you have been given permission to search for a private house dump. The owner should first be questioned if there any records in the family or farm archives where rubbish was dumped. If not, were there any old ponds which were filled in during the Victorian era or any quarries filled in? No, O.K. Where would you state looking?

Let's talk common-sense first. If the house is on a hill-side, it would not make sense to drive a horse and cart full of rubbish uphill. Secondly the household rubbish would not be put outside in a bin through the front door. It would be taken out through the kitchen door. Has the kitchen always been where it is now? In large houses, alterations through the centuries are constant. We will, therefore, start looking from the kitchen door. If on a slope, we would start looking for a dump downhill. Otherwise we start looking for signs of a dump, the wasteland test with nettles, brambles, elderberry bushes may still apply here, but not necessarily so, as sometimes soil may have been dumped on top, compressed over the years, and could now have become ploughed land. I would certain do some test-digging in small woodland areas and check out the soil in nearby ploughed fields.

Rare cottage-shaped ink bottle

There is no quick and easy method of finding an old country house dump. But for those with the energy to try, one thing is certain. Any house built in its own grounds before say, 1880, will have its own private dump. And if the house is 17th or 18th century, the rewards are even more attractive. Very few have ever been searched as the owners are unlikely to even consider the question of old rubbish. They are usually very busy gentleman-farmers, businessmen, stockbrokers, lawyers or judges etc. Why would they want to be digging in old rubbish dumps? Thousands, if not tens of thousands of these dumps exist. It will not be easy, but it's up to you, the searcher, to try.

STILL NOWHERE TO DIG?

I am intentionally repeating the following sentence. Victorian refuse is all around us. So far I have mentioned various places we can search for it. There are tens of thousands of small wooded areas dotted around the country. Have you spotted the remains of a metal bathtub with a tree growing around it? That's a dump. Many quarries are dumped in; old farms and country houses all have a Victorian dump and possibly an 18th century one. There are also sites of demolished old houses which have yet to be built over, usually in the countryside. There are bulldozers all over the land ripping up the soil to make new motorways and building new estates. Keep your eye on these. There are rivers, canals and creeks with brickworks on their banks, at least in the south of England. Get talking to people who can point the way to a dump for you: farmers, country house owners, bulldozer drivers and road-makers, allotment holders and old men lurking in pub corners.

Everyone can say they do not know where to go digging. What they really mean is that they do not know of an open dump which they can just drive to and dig without any effort to find it. Opened dumps are soon dug out. Even if you had such a dump today, in a few weeks or a few months time it would be exhausted. You would then have to find a new dump. Or are you waiting for someone else to find it for you? You need to get out there once a week to find a dump. Make it a habit. It's a day out in the fresh air. Take the wife and kids if you have them and make it a day out for the family. Take some food and call it a picnic. Use the tips I have given you. Try talking to farmers or country house owners. Make a list of places to search before you go out. There are many places to look.

Many old dumps were badly dug in the 1970s and 80s. Weekend diggers were only there for one day. They dug down as far as time allowed and possibly filled in the hole. Few dug to the ultimate depth of the refuse. And if they did, they threw the soil from their trench on to land which had not been dug and it probably still hasn't because people assumed it had, with a loose pile of soil and ash on top of it. I would stick my neck out and state that I am certain that no council dump that has ever been opened has been completely emptied of its finds, unless a mechanical digger and half-a-dozen searchers were on hand. Re-digging a once-dug dump means shifting a lot of soil or ash, but if you want finds you cannot be worried at the thought of some physical work. It's good for you. And don't ever give up.

Back in the early 1970s, the very first dump I found lasted two years and between two of us we found over 500 pot-lids. It was a large dump and was London refuse, ideal for pot-lids. After this we stopped counting. This was a dump which provided me with nine or ten submarine poison bottles. In this site we encountered water at about 18 inches as it was near a tidal creek. The waterlogged bottles were often "sick," discoloured by water action. Beware when buying bottles at fairs as some unscrupulous people oil these sick bottles which makes them look O.K. until the oil dries up. Of course other people soon arrived on the site and the haul of pot-lids and submarine poison bottles from this one field was very high over the period. We were spoilt in those days as we did not have to search for new dumps. We only did so as a break from London refuse on occasions as after digging for a few years, there were few surprises. The pot-lids and the bottles we found were not local and digging up the same finds did become boring at times. Oh how we were spoilt! We left behind dumps where digging was uncomfortable and under-water as we could not keep the glassware, only the pot-lids and it was so easy to find somewhere easier to dig the next day.

Use the fork to loosen soil around special finds to avoid damage

When I was digging full-time I never went to the large dump on Sundays as I had my auctions to attend to. I would have avoided the place on Sundays anyway because all the week-enders came: people who worked during the week and dug on Sundays only. I left the dump to them, their wives and children and they dug big holes for me. On Monday mornings I could walk around the site where the digging was (it moved every week) and picked up all the Bovril jars and glass and stone ink bottles as many people left them behind. They were so numerous, but I had an American customer who visited me monthly and I sold him a holdall full for 25p each. He took them on the plane with him to New York and paid excess baggage and still made a profit. (I must point out that he did not just visit England for the ink bottles. He was here on other business.) The weekenders were very kind to me. Many of them left nice deep holes up to six-feet deep. It was easy to jump in and continue raking out the goodies on Monday mornings from a solid wall of Victorian refuse.

Re-digging dumps which were badly dug over thirty or so years ago will obviously not yield as many finds as they did the first time around and it will necessitate some hard digging. Nevertheless, I remember those days well when dumps were easy to find and we just dug a hole as far as we could in one day, without reaching the bottom of the refuse. Think about this if you have nowhere to dig, providing the land is not now built over. I also remember that new diggers did not see half of the small items: miniature or small pot-lids, ointment pots, dolls heads and china limbs they threw out on their shovels but a sieve would have found these.

I used to know a man who walked out into shallow rivers wearing waders feeling for old bottles underwater near bridges. He found them too, usually just downstream of the bridge. And he couldn't even swim. I believe he is still alive as far as I know. And I have found old bottles at the bottom of my own garden, in farm walls and under floorboards in empty old houses.

So when I hear someone say "I have nowhere to dig," I would ask: "What are you doing about it?" Nobody is going to find your dump for you. I am an old man now and cannot dig, but I am still interested and have been recently become involved in discussions with the owners of old mansion houses. They are usually affluent people and also very busy. They know nothing about refuse or about the interesting and valuable contents of early material. Like many people, some think that the collection of refuse is something which has always existed. Some never even think about refuse. It is up to us to educate them about old dumps. Admittedly there is the danger that they will turn your proposal down and do the digging themselves or have their farm-workers do it. But this is a chance you have to take. One idea would be to write a leaflet about old private house-dumps as a sort of business proposal, offering to share the proceeds of your digging with them. They may be able to help you with any information about possible landfill sites near their house. They are all sitting on valuable dumps and they don't know it. If you approach them in a businesslike way, politely and discreetly, you may be invited to dig there.

And if the tens of thousands of dumps in the U.K. are not enough for you, what about Europe? France and Belgium are not that far away and to the best of my knowledge, dump-digging never really took off on the Continent. I remember an old friend of mine, Roy Morgan who used to live in Wellingborough once obtained some beautifully coloured Codds and Hamiltons in amber, green and even cobalt blue from Belgium or France many years ago. I have also seen some very collectable French pot-lids over the years. Many English people have bought houses in France in recently. Have you a friend or relative who lives there? Fancy a holiday with them? Take your digging boots.

I believe that for overseas diggers to be allowed to dig dumps in France or anywhere else on the Continent, a special approach would be required. French farmers (if they own the land containing the dump) are not known to be very co-operative. But on the other hand they would not turn their backs on a lump sum. I think the only way this could work is for a few people to form a small conglomerate and use a mechanical digger to extract the finds. Of course, test-digging would have to be done first to establish the age and value of the finds. To prevent others digging there, extraction would have to be done as quickly as possible, with the diggers living locally or even camping on site. A group of four or five people could accomplish this, but of course it would only be worthwhile if the material was of the period required, say 1880 to 1920.Research would be necessary to establish when dumping first began in the area. The idea needs some local investigation overseas first of course, but this is only a suggestion for when you really cannot find anywhere in the U.K.

I have often ruminated about India. Consider in the days of the Raj when English army officers and their families lived in the hill stations and had all their luxury food items sent out by Harrods and other large London stores who specialised in this army business. What has happened to all the printed pot-lids exported to these army families? Many proud stiff upper-lipped British officers must have used bear's grease on their hair and these are the rarer more valuable types of lids. I realise that to find these dumps is probably impractical, but I can't help wondering and pondering. Another friend of mine, Greg Payne, editor of *Treasure Hunting* magazine for many years, once went to India for a holiday. In Delhi he discovered a Street of Bottle-Sellers. He bought a few 1920s type ginger beers there. He found that they were still making and using Codd bottles in the 1970s and he ordered a load to be shipped over to England. They were aqua coloured with black marbles and had straw packed in the necks to stop the rattle. They were sold extremely cheaply over there and sold well in England, being in mint condition. India may still have its old army rubbish dumps, but it's a long, long way to go for a dig. But enough of this ruminating!

Dump-digging began in the U.S. in the 1950s with the excavation of early frontier towns which had been abandoned and it is still really big business there. Of course it soon spread to Canada and then we started here around 1970. Australia is now also very much into old bottles and pot-lids as is New Zealand. I cannot say what the digging situation is in South Africa, although I know there are collectors there. It would appear that dump-digging is mainly confined to English-speaking countries. I do not travel overseas much, so I cannot say what the dump-digging situation is on the Continent.

CHAPTER FIVE

On Finding Your Dump

Finding an un-dug rubbish dump takes a certain amount of know-how. It takes time, often much leg-work and some travelling expense. When you do find one, it is imperative that you are able to keep it for your own use as long as possible. In many cases, however, you may leave your dump on the second or third day to return next morning to find visitors also digging there.

Considering the high value of a dump, their scarcity and the amount of time you have given to finding it, would you advertise it in the local newspaper to invite dozens of other collector-diggers to share it with you? Of course not. But I know of many people who have done so unwittingly, so read on.

Do not park your car in a country lane alongside your new-found dump. Leave your car in the nearest village or at least somewhere in a lay-by. Don't be afraid to do a little walking to and from the dump. You may think that no-one will think anything about seeing your car parked in the middle of nowhere. Don't you believe it! I would certainly be inquisitive if I saw this and would probably investigate it—or at least I would have done years ago before my legs retired. I have actually found someone else's dump this way by spotting such a car.

Even without the car parking, news will spread like dandelion seeds in the wind. Digger-collectors can smell a newly opened dump. People take their dogs for a walk in country places, especially through woodland. They have eyes to see the diggings. Word spreads that somebody is digging in a wood and before you know what has happened you will find that your new-found dump is swarming with strangers and it will be emptied out very quickly.

Secondly, although you may wish to share your dump with your digging partner (always a good idea) you should *not* discuss it in pubs or anywhere for that matter. Also, do not be in a hurry to sell your finds as I know to my cost. Mineral bottles, ginger beers and pot-lids may have town names on them, which act as a signpost for people miles away, telling them which area you are digging in. And an experienced digger, once he knows there is an opened dump in a town or village, will easily find it.

Unless the dump is very small, the chances of you keeping a largish dump to yourself until it is completely dug out are very small. I have mentioned one or two precautions you can take, but if you are digging on a site for a couple of weeks or more, the chances are that you will soon be joined by other diggers. There is little you can do if this happens and there is no point in becoming aggressive. However, if you have permission from the landowner and the others have not, that is a different situation and requires attention. By and large, you can only take the best precautions to keep your dump secret and then keep your fingers crossed. If you have done all you can, that is all you can do.

After a day's digging, always cave in the sides of a deep hole. The reasons are three-fold. It releases more finds for you to take home. Secondly, anyone strolling through the woods or field will immediately spot the layers of pottery and glass in the pit you have left. Lastly, leaving a big hole is dangerous, especially for children and animals and you don't wish to give anyone an excuse to complain to the police. Leaving a deep hole in a public place is irresponsible. It does not take long to shovel out the loose material next morning.

Transfer-printed ginger
beer bottle

Railway interest ginger
beer bottle

Two ginger-beer bottles with pictorial trademarks

Finally, if you have found an un-dug dump, dig there every day. Try to empty it as quickly as possible. If you work, take a few days off if you can. Every day you leave your opened dump, each day is another chance for someone else to find it.

PERMISSION TO DIG?

All land is owned by someone, even what appears to be a small piece of wasteland. All dump-diggers know that they should really obtain permission before digging on someone else's land. Whatever relics are underground are the property of the landowner and taking them away is theft, even if he thinks they are just a load of old rubbish, which they are! Usually the landowner will know of the existence of the dump but has no idea it has a cash value.

In my experience most farmers do not welcome anyone digging on their waste-land and rightly so. I have encountered two who were happy for us to dig in their woods after explaining what was interesting about the old bottles and after giving them one or two of their own bottles. Most of my digging years were on a brickworks site, as I have already mentioned, several hundred acres in extent. There the owners tolerated us for years, providing we kept away from their working areas during working hours, which we did. The works were yards away from the River Medway, a tidal river. When someone ripped down the sea-wall to dig out the pot-lids in it and flooded the offices of the brickworks at high tide, they were not too happy. And in time, due to the high incidence of accidents on the site, it was gradually lost to us by building and being fenced in. There is today nowhere worth digging there. In a wooded area, where refuse has been dumped in a hollow and trees allowed to grow through it, once dug out Nature does not like empty spaces and soon fills them in and no harm has been done. I suspect that most diggers have dug such sites without permission and have had no complaints from landowners. I know I have. These are usually small patches of virtual wasteland. However, on larger sites, full-blown town dumps, these are a different story. I don't know what other people have done, but personally I have continued to dig there until told otherwise. In all my years of digging I have only been ordered off a site once and this was not in a wood In a few cases the owners of a piece of land which contained a dump, have capitalised on the demand for old bottles and pot-lids by charging a small fee to diggers. Many years ago this was only £1 a day. Today, of course, this would have to be much more if such a dump were found. This is the same system as buying a day ticket to fish in a lake, where the landowner comes round every morning and afternoon and sells you a day-ticket. This is a good way to operate and no-one would object to paying a reasonable daily fee for the pleasure of digging a dump. Everybody gains. It's a pity others don't emulate this system. In one instance I know of, the farmer earned more money from his unploughable land than he would have if growing a crop. In the U.S.A. where dump finds have a higher value than in the U.K., such landowners earn significantly more.

If there is livestock in a field of refuse, again, there is some danger to the animals if the refuse is exposed. It would be irresponsible to dig in these circumstances. But in general, if there is no livestock and if you are not walking across ploughed land, you would be doing no damage or putting man or beast at risk.

I always advise people to take someone with them on digging expeditions. Take your wife or some other digging partner for several reasons. When you become excited at a rare find, you have no-one to enthuse to. Such moments are too precious and should be shared. It is certainly more pleasant to have company when digging, but also it is safer in case of an accident. You could have a cave-in in a deep hole. You could cut your hands or legs badly on protruding pieces of glass, pottery or metal. Anything could happen and it is wise to take a first-aid pack with you. Always ensure you have something to drink and a snack. Take your digging tools, a garden fork and spade. I always take a few sheets of old newspaper in a strong holdall or back-pack in which to wrap special finds such as dolls' heads, pot-lids and special bottles. Fill your bag with the commoner or stronger bottles and keep the wrapped delicate goodies on top.

1920s & 1930s DUMPS—ARE THEY WORTH DIGGING?

Yes, they are. You are not likely to find any pot-lids in dumps of this date, although you may find one or two late ones which were continued as a prestige novelty after most had gone out of use. Although the value of a dump is often rated by the number of pot-lids found, other saleable items can be found.

Glass bottles from this period will not be mouth-blown, being made by the A.B.M. process (automatic blowing machine) with seams all the way up to and over the lip, i.e. made in one piece. Nevertheless some colourful blue and green or brown poison bottles will be plentiful from these days, as will the large fat dumpy Bovril jars. Stone ginger-beers were still in use during this time, although they may not all be blob-top, possibly champagne-shaped. There will be no Hamiltons, but there should still be some Codds. I have found the largest bisque dolls heads as big as Jaffa oranges came from these late dumps and these are very saleable.

Occasionally metal enamelled signs can be found in these dumps, often with some rusty corners, but still with an auction value. There are specialist sales for these. One fact which is not always considered is that in these between-the-wars dumps, sometimes earlier items from the Edwardian period are found, although this cannot be guaranteed. These would have been discarded at a later date, possibly during a house clearance. One other point to remember here is that although you may be finding 1920s material or even later, the dump may deeper down or at one end, have been commenced earlier, so you need to ensure that you dig to the very bottom of your refuse in case it is Edwardian deeper down. Having discussed all the places to search for your dump, you should now be ready to start digging.

CHAPTER SIX

Digging Safely & Efficiently

The dump you intend to dig will be one of two kinds: it will be level with the surrounding land, possibly in a wood, but not necessarily so, or it will be a gigantic council dump heaped up six to ten-feet higher than surrounding land. Where do you start?

Many beginner diggers just dive in to make finds in one spot and then start a new hole next day. It is important after you have taken the trouble to find your dump that you dig down to the bottom of the refuse, to the clay or sub-soil. Refuse material which has been buried for about a century or more is usually compressed but still friable, often with layers of brown (metal rust) and grey (coal ash). You will know when you reach the bottom. On brickworks dumps it would be impossible to dig with a spade or shovel as the fine ash had been sieved out and the material in which we were digging was fairly solid pottery and glass. A shovel or spade here was only useful to scrape out the bottom of the hole when loose material was piling up there. On other town dumps, there is much black soil and using a fork to loosen the material is first necessary as a spade can easily break a valuable bottle. Loosen the soil with the fork and use the tines to prise open the wall of refuse you expose. Prise and probe with the fork only. If you do whack your fork through the middle of a rare pot-lid or bottle, be assured you will not be the first!

When you throw out material from your digging with your spade, do not simply throw it without checking what's on it. This sounds an obvious statement, but I have seen people digging furiously and throwing out the loose stuff without checking what they were throwing away. Spread it out as you throw it and check the fall-out from each load as you could be throwing out a small pot-lid and covering it over with the next load. If you have a digging partner you could share this task. To avoid throwing your soil on top of un-dug refuse, start at the very extreme edge of the refuse and throw the soil on to soil that does not contain anything. You know where the refuse starts by test digging to find the edge. *On every dump I have worked on I have seen people digging and throwing the contents of their trench out on to un-dug refuse.* This wastes about a third of your dump and they are too precious to waste. Similarly if you are also digging three-feet down into six-feet of refuse, you are also wasting half of it. (It is for this reason that I believe many dumps dug out years ago would probably repay another dig.) Not everybody has time on a Sunday to dig down six feet. I realise that hobby diggers have only a limited time to spend digging at the weekend and digging is hard work if you are not accustomed to it. If you are digging on a dump that has already been started, throw your soil out only on the side that has already been dug and dig into the solid side. To prevent fall-in, occasionally it will be necessary to rake loose material this back from the edge of your hole, especially if digging deep.

Most people, when they are nearly ready to pack up, stick their forks into the overhang and cave the wall of refuse into the hole to make a few last-minute finds. This is fine, but don't forget that all that loose material is covering over more goodies if you have not reached the bottom. Because most diggers are hobby diggers and have only a few hours to spend on the site, it is unavoidable that such bad digging practices occur and I am not blaming anybody. For the professional who digs every day as I did, I could start late in the morning and work until early evening, leaving my hole *not* filled-in overnight so that I could jump in again next morning.(providing it was not dangerous to others) Do not dig yourself into a small round hole. It is far safer and more productive to dig a long trench. I have sometimes known people to have dug themselves into a deep hole without considering how they are going to get out. Twice I remember hearing a voice calling out

"Is there anybody there? Help! Is there anybody there?" On investigation I have had to pull the person out of a deep hole on the handle end of my fork. Leave a step if you are going to dig eight feet straight down!

I used to have a digging friend who was very stockily-built, short arms and short legs, the ideal physique for work of this kind. He would spend the first two hours digging out a hole about six-feet deep by eight-feet square. He was like a mechanical shovel, having very big biceps and strong as an ox. During this digging he had a boy with him, checking all that was thrown out of the hole by spreading it, whilst he was not looking for finds himself, although he did encounter some, obviously. He left the main searching to his boy on top who was also pushing the soil back away from the hole as he checked it. The eight feet-square hole was only dug three-feet deep half-way across the hole and then six-feet to the bottom of the refuse. This was his step to exit the hole. Once the hole was dug he would stop for half-an hour to examine his finds and have a drink and a snack before starting again. Now that all the hard work was done, he only had to probe into the solid wall of refuse in the six-foot hole at a leisurely pace, careful not to break any lids or bottles. Before finishing for the day he would fork over the "step" he had left and turn that over into the six-foot hole so that he still had a step to climb out on. He found more lids, bottles and dolls heads than anyone I know and he always dug out 100% of his hole.

DON'T BECOME A TROGLODYTE

I have seen people in deep holes making caves into the wall of refuse and digging further and further into it until they have their heads underneath about a ton of soil and refuse! I have also seen the ambulance there three times. Digging caves into unreliable friable refuse is not a wise decision. The cave-ins that trapped people underground have done much harm, and I once read about one fatal accident in England where a young boy had been trapped and suffocated when his hole collapsed on him.

I think what happens is that once you have dug your deep hole and you can sit down or squat at leisure to poke out your finds, people get carried away with enthusiasm and just keep on digging a cave. If you're not careful you'll be carried away by an ambulance. Instead, you should stand up and knock down the top of your overhang occasionally so that there is no cave. It means you have to stop finding and start digging out again, but at least it's safe that way. Be careful to keep the sides of your hole straight. Do not allow it to taper with an overhang or you might find yourself with a guest in your hole if a neighbouring digger decides to come and say hello. I have known this to happen too.

This man is digging himself into a lot of trouble. The rubble is already falling back in the hole. He has not considered how to extract himself from this 8ft. hole and he has started a cave deep down. Note: he is using a coking fork as he is digging under water.

Work laterally so that your trench stretches sideways across the dump reaching the empty soil at both ends eventually. If you have to dig down only two or three feet, you will not be in any danger from cave-ins, but if you have to dig six-feet or more down to reach the bottom, don't forget you have to get out of this deep hole sometime. A long trench is preferable to a round hole.

Some dumps (mainly woodland) have no covering and the bottles are nearly peeping out of the soil. However on brickworks and council dumps they are often sealed in with soil or clay to a depth of about 18 inches to deter vermin and prevent smells. When starting to dig a new dump, don't forget this and walk away if you don't find bottles immediately under the grass.

In dumps which are close to rivers and creeks, you may often encounter water in your hole at a certain depth. I have had to contend with this in several parts of a dump, but fortunately the water does not damage pot-lids although it does damage glassware. The only harm it might cause pot-lids is to fill the crazing in with brown rust marks. (see chapter on cleaning finds) One particular site was waterlogged at six inches but it was very productive of pot-lids. We were all finding three to five a session. A normal garden fork was of little use here, so we found that by using a coking fork with about 12 or more tines, we could lift out the finds easier as the tines were closer together. These are used in coal-yards.

To summarise: try always to dig to the bottom of the refuse and do not cover over un-dug land. And *do not dig caves.*

CHAPTER SEVEN

Let's Go Digging

What's a typical day's digging like? And what are we likely to find? For the benefit of newcomers to digging, I cannot take you out individually, so perhaps we can share a short session on paper. Let's just use our imagination . . .

We'll make an early start, about 8 a.m. when the dump is quiet. A previous digger has left a nice big hole here, although he's caved the sides in, we can soon dig this out and start again. We'll shovel out all this loose stuff onto the other pile of loose stuff and I'll just make some room for it by pulling this mound away from the edge of the hole. Don't forget to turn round as you shovel and check what you're throwing away. It should only take half-an-hour to clear this hole, and then we can start checking that solid wall of refuse for finds. It's not a big hole, only about three feet deep, but we'll dig in the bottom in a minute to see how far down it goes.

Look out—there's a bottle coming up. Dark green and round with embossing on the base. Oh yes, that's a Hunyadi Janos bottle for spring water from Budapest. Pity they didn't emboss the sides of the bottle, but they had colourful paper labels on the sides instead. See that German writing on the underside, "Bitterquelle." I think that means bitter-spring. You'll find a few of these dumpy-necked bottles and all have the name of the spring town on the base. "K" means it's from Karlsbad, for example. They're all from Continental springs. I believe they are called aperients. Not worth much, but if you're just beginning, they're attractive bottles with dimpled marks on the glass. They're called whittle marks transferred from the wooden moulds they're made in.

Ron & Mrs. D on a Dagenham brickworks site

Be careful you don't miss any small dolls head and shoulders when you're shovelling out. These types are glazed and are black and white with a touch of pink on the cheeks. The larger and better types have open-top heads and are made of unglazed bisque porcelain, usually with German makers' names on the back of the head. If you find one of those, don't throw away the soil from inside the head without checking the swivel eyes are still there. Often they are. That's a stoneware jam-pot, the off-white one with ridges on its side. If you look underneath, you'll see the lighthouse trademark for Hartley's. Not really worth taking. Now we've shovelled out all the loose stuff from the last digging, we can use the fork to go a bit deeper and then we can have a short break. The beauty of this work is that you can stop when you feel like a rest. Sitting on a pile of broken pottery and glass from people's dustbins isn't everyone's idea of comfort. But once you're hot and sweaty and you've got your hands dirty, a cup of tea tastes beautiful and facing you now is a wall about six-feet long and four feet

high of untouched compressed Victorian rubbish. The hole is now clear
of debris and we're ready to start finding something decent. Anticipation
is high and we are the only people on the dump. Nice and peaceful, no
loud radios, no barking dogs. We'll start again now. You are going to come
across lots of shells in the rubbish. The Victorians loved their shell-fish.

If you spot what looks like a pot-lid, be careful to push your fork in a
few inches away and prise it out gently. Look, there's a plain white pot-lid.
They're the ones that just had paper labels on them. No, we don't want to
keep it, but I usually keep the bases if they're not chipped. We can often
match up a printed lid with a base, but this is not really necessary as the
lids are collected as they are. Are the bases all the same? No. The tops
are different shapes and the bases mirror the shape of the top. If the top
is mushroom shaped, like Gosnell's toothpaste for example which has an
overhanging ridge, the base will also look like an upside down mushroom.
Watch out, there's another lid! Prise it out carefully. Oh it's a Burgess's
Anchovy Paste, one of the most common. Only worth a few pounds, but
it's in good order. There you are—your first pot-lid. You'll always remember
your first lid. Mine was a green Gosnell's toothpaste with Queen Victoria's
head on it. Don't stare at it all day. You'll wear it out. If it wasn't so common
I guess we'd value it as a pictorial lid, as it has the royal coat-of-arms on it.
There's a pipe-bowl there by your foot. See, it has Queen Victoria's head
on one side and King Edward's on the other side. Probably done for the
Coronation, so that helps to date the site, about 1902. That one you're
pulling out is a brown salt-glazed blacking bottle. Fairly common, again,
but they look good in the kitchen with a few flowers inside. Careful when
you wash that out at home. They usually make a black mess of your sink.
Now that fancy flask-shaped bottle is special. Careful—pull it out, don't
let fall or it might break. Yes it is thick glass. It's a brown Warner's Safe
Cure, an American quack medicine. Some are green, some are brown, and
there are two sizes. That's the smaller one. Worth keeping as they're well
collected. See that picture of a safe embossed on it. That's their trade mark.
Quack medicine bottles are well collected, so that's a keeper. Wrap it safely
before you put it in the bag.

Looks like rain coming on. Let's call it a day for now. Just a short session, I know, but enough for your first day. You've got a bag full of fairly common bottles, a few glass inks, a pot-lid, a Coronation pipe bowl and a Warner's. Also you have several small salt-glazed bottles for bluing and polishes. Not bad for a couple of hours. Not a good haul, but good enough. Is your back aching? Don't worry, the more you do, the easier it gets. Rip down the bank now and you'll be able to fill up your bag with a few more finds before we go home. With more practice you'll eventually be able to dig for up to four hours and you'll be taking home three or four pot-lids every time as long as you're digging in Victorian or Edwardian material. Then you'll be a dump-digger.

CHAPTER EIGHT

Collecting

In every county or state there is at least one bottle-collecting club which any dump-digger can join. The words "bottle-collecting" have a wide meaning, as some collectors are more interested in pot-lids than bottles, with others fascinated by decorated clay pipe bowls and others specialising in stone ginger-beer bottles. The hobby encompasses all of these, as all are found in old refuse dumps of a hundred years old or more and some people collect all the range.

Inevitably you will find many duplicated items and after you have chosen finds for your own private collection you will have dozens of items for sale. There are two methods to dispose of these. For the more valuable items such as pot-lids and rare bottles there are several specialist auctions and these can be found online. Alternatively you can auction them yourself on e-bay, provided that you describe them accurately, mentioning all faults, chips and stains if they exist. The more common items such as ink bottles, Bovril and other beef extracts, salt-glaze pots and jars can be either sold by the boxful in general auctions or if you wish to take a stall at car-boot sales or at specialist bottle fairs, this is another way to dispose of the more commonly found items. Often dealers are willing to buy boxes of such finds at a price which allows them to sell them off individually. Check online for bottle fairs, auctions and your local club. Also I would advise you to subscribe to an antique bottle magazine currently being published to keep abreast of what is happening in the world of collecting. (*Antique*

Bottle Collector is an excellent U.K. quarterly and there are several in the U.S.A. and Australia) Such magazines cover pot-lids and other finds in addition to bottles. Find these online.

Mrs. D finds a pot-lid

Pot-lids and transfer-printed food pots like cream jars, paste pots and cure-all ointment pots etc. come under the umbrella of advertising and packaging antiques or *advertiques*. Also do the quack cure-all medicine and tonic bottles of bye-gone days. To some degree also under this heading are ginger-beer bottles and embossed mineral water and beer bottles, especially those with attractive pictorial trademarks. Some people collect anything to do with beer and brewing, *breweriana*, and they buy old beer bottles, whisky and water jugs, match-strikers and advertising ashtrays and this is a separate branch of collecting. Clay pipes bowls with decorated bowls are also collected. Collectors would obviously prefer to own the complete pipe, but is rare to find one of these in a dump. Some of the more valuable large pipe bowls have been manufactured in recent times, using old moulds, so if you see complete figural pipes for sale as white as snow and clean as a whistle, you will recognise them for what they are. This does not mean you should not collect them, but dug pipes rarely come out of the ground in mint condition and complete. You should know that such pipes are modern and pay accordingly. The range of pipe bowls is amazing. They were often given away by publicans and they acted as a form of advertising. Those with the head of King Edward VII may have come from the *Kings Head* pub and those with a dog on one side and a gun on the other came from . . . you guessed it, *the Dog & Gun* pub. But there are many fascinating clay pipe decorations and this is only one branch of the collectable finds you encounter in old dumps.

You can see, therefore, that the interest in old bottles, lids and pipes is not only just confined to the dump-digging fraternity. Also, if you have local finds you can sell these to local historians and I have often been able to return whisky flasks and beer bottles and pipe bowls back to the pubs they started life in a century ago. When I lived in Kent I found a few Shepherd Neame beer bottles which went back to the original brewery museum in Faversham and the 1p glass whisky flasks that customers bought from their local pubs also have a local interest, often naming the landlord as well as the pub on their flat sides. These were filled from the barrel and carried home by their customers in their hip-pockets. The bisque china dolls heads I found were bought mainly by lady dealers and these were eventually re-made into dolls again. Since digging started in the U.K. about 1970, the number of Victorian and Edwardian dolls in existence has increased enormously due to the phenomenon of dump-digging. And I had several lady dealers at my stall in Bermondsey Antique Market waiting for my arrival there every Friday morning to snap up all the heads and china limbs I had found that week. You can therefore see that there are several outlets for your surplus finds. You will always finish up with many of the commonest items, but as they are from a period long ago and no more are being made, you will find that you dispose of them all eventually. The public will buy the jagged-top cheaply made ink bottles for their crudeness and eccentric necks, often full of air bubbles. They are not valuable although the unusual colours and varieties are. Similarly with the numerous dolly-blue or bluing bottles in brown stoneware, small cylindrical bottles I used to pick up off the dump on Monday mornings as the weekenders usually left them behind. Most finds will sell, eventually if the price is right. I have met people who said they dug for profit only, as in a way I did myself as it was my living for many years, but I do not believe you can dig dumps *just* for the money. You must enjoy it, love it even. And every digger becomes a collector. To obtain a free collection of antique relics and earn a profit from your duplicates is an ideal situation—and you also gain the thrill and pleasure of digging up your own antiques. Dump-digging in my humble opinion is the ultimate hobby.

For beginners who wish to know more about the fascinating world of dump finds, there is a wide array of books to cover specialist areas of collecting: advertising relics, which includes pot-lids, mineral water bottles and their ingenious range of inventions made in the 19th century to keep the carbon dioxide in fizzy drink bottles, clay pipes, dolls heads, breweriana etc. Just check online if you wish to see the rarities and variety under "Antique Bottles for Sale" or "Pot-lids for Sale" and also on e-bay. You might be amazed to see how much these throw-away items from somebody's dustbin are selling for today. I cannot possibly show many illustrations of these in this humble effort, but whatever your specialist interest, I guarantee you will find a book on the subject.

Very rare submarine poison bottle.
These now reach £800 to £1,000 in auctions

My last word must unfortunately mention fakes. With the rarer bottles and pot-lids realising several hundred £s and some thousands, fakes are an inevitable but distasteful subject. If you are digging up your own collectables, there is no problem. But for beginners I would advise you NOT to buy any rare high-priced items of any kind until you have familiarised yourself with genuine old bottles and pot-lids. Join a club, attend fairs; handle as many pieces as you can. No seasoned dump digger would fall into the trap of buying a bear's grease lid which has been recently stencilled on to a plain white lid and varnished over. A rare black and white bear's grease lid recently sold for over £5,000. You will easily spot a fake when you have seen and handled the genuine item. Check online for your local club and news of bottle fairs.

When I ran my auctions for dump-finds, most lots were bought by dealers from London with a few collectors buying individual items. The lots were sold on behalf of local digger-collectors in Kent and the auctions continued for six years until I left the area. At this time many common lids were selling for £1 or £2, most others at £3 or £4 with a rare bear's grease lid at £30 being the top price realised for a lid. Green Gosnell's toothpaste lids adorned with Queen Victoria's young head sold at £5 or £6. Submarine poison bottles sold for just a few pounds and cottage ink bottles for £20 to £30 with £50 for a cobalt blue example. This was in the 1970s, of course. The value of common items has hardly risen in recent years, but those of rare items have multiplied many times. I am somewhat out of touch with auction prices of today, but a rare bottle will always be rare and valuable. People who kept their collection could not have had a better investment, especially if they were all self-dug.

The phenomenon of digging up old refuse has created a new and exciting hobby for people from all walks of life. Furthermore, it endows an interest in history to many thousands of people who never considered the past before. It has brought history into their kitchens and living rooms. There are many thousands of homes now where Victorian blacking pots are used for flower vases and where Victorian and Edwardian toothpaste and bear's grease lids adorn the walls. It has also enabled many to collect these antiquities which they could not otherwise have afforded. Dump-digging has brought antique collecting to the man-in-the-street.

CHAPTER NINE

Cleaning Your Finds

Bottles and other finds which have been buried underground for a century or more are sometimes stained or damaged in some other way. It is surprising that any are found complete, but they are. Glass mineral and beer bottles of a century ago were much thicker and stronger than modern ones.

It is important to remember that collectors always prefer undamaged relics. Some collectors have become quite proficient at restoring damaged finds for their own collection and if a perfect specimen is not available, that's fine. Clay pipes are the exception as nearly all are damaged. The decorated bowls are collected with just a short piece of stem remaining.

Glassware suffers the most underground, mainly by the action of water. When a glass bottle is lifted from wet soil it may appear to be clean and transparent, but when dry it may have acquired a greyish colour and will not be transparent. This is called "glass sickness" and cannot be cured. Underground water gradually eats away at the surface of the glass and reacting with the soda content, it leaves behind the skeletal remains of a layer or more of glass. This can often flake away when handled. This causes light to be refracted into rainbow colours. In extreme cases such as in Roman glass or even 17th century onion wine bottles, this opalescence is attractive and may not detract from the bottle's value, but for Victorian and Edwardian glass bottles, such "sick" bottles are not normally collected unless they are rare. I have already mentioned the warning about bottles which have been smeared with oil or varnish, which has the effect of making them appear wet, which then causes the sickness to temporarily disappear. But it does not disappear as it will become visible once the oil or varnish has gone. It is considered dishonest to sell "sick" bottles disguised with a coating of oil or varnish without informing the buyer, but if a collector wishes to varnish his own, that's fine. If suspicious about a bottle offered for sale, give it a good sniff. There is no real cure for this problem and only rare specimens are worth keeping. Where the problem is only slight and is confined to one small area, jeweller's rouge, a fine abrasive powder, can help but only with mild glass sickness. Where the structure of the glass is breaking down and crumbling, there is nothing to be done. Jeweller's rouge can also help with small patches of brown rust on printed pots of stone ginger beers, after removal of any solid lumps of rust.

But first, before we do anything, we have to wash all our finds. This can cause domestic strife and even threaten marriages, as there is much goo, smell and sometimes wildlife inside old bottles. For marital harmony, outside washing is suggested and use hot, soapy water, with a range of bottle brushes. Be more vigilant with the blue, green and brown poison bottles as the action of hot water on poisonous contents, even after a century, can give off strong fumes. Similarly stoneware blacking bottles and ink bottles may sometimes have dried contents and although non-toxic they can make a mess in a sink. Sometimes ants, beetles, grubs and worms are found in old bottles, so be warned not to ask your wife to do the washing for you. I once found baby slow-worms inside a stoneware blacking bottle and although they gave my wife a fright as she thought they were snakes, they are quite harmless.

Once dried out, I usually wipe the finds over with an old dry towel. To give the bottles a high gloss, a spray of Mr. Sheen or similar glass cleaner and a wipe-over afterwards will make them sparkle. On bottles of unusual shape, such as small ink bottles, a small teapot-spout brush is ideal as it can easily be bent to reach out of the way corners. For stubborn marks or deposits inside larger glass bottles, a quantity of rough sand mixed with a small amount of water and swished around is very effective for internal bottle cleaning.

Dolls heads should be washed very carefully, especially the unglazed bisque pink heads. Check inside before washing if you have not done so at the dump for loose swivel eyes, sometimes found still inside the heads. Do not use any kind of chemicals on the heads as this will take away the colouring. Dolls heads are finished off by hand-painting: the eyebrows, cheek rouge and lips and this is a skilled job, best left to the doll restorers who may be the eventual buyer. The smaller black and white glazed head and shoulders should wash up well, but these may also need facial colours repainted. Do not use any kind of scourer pad on any doll's head as this will remove the hand-painting and reduce the value.

Clay pipes, if grey from smoke or heat in the ashes, can be immersed in bleach to whiten them, but only for a short time. They must afterwards be placed in a bowl of water for a few days immediately after to prevent the bleach dissolving the pipe-clay. Do not use extra-powerful bleach or leave the pipes in it too long. Brown rust stains on pipes can be removed by a liquid rust-remover called Jenolite which I use on pot-lids for removing the brown rust stains in the crazing.

Here again, care must be taken as the liquid is an acid. My method is to use it for soaking pot-lids first as it is expensive. Then I re-use it for pipes afterwards, as it loses strength by exposure to air. Brown rust on pot-lids is usually easy to remove using the pink liquid, Jenolite. Sometimes the brown disappears within two or three hours and sometimes they need to be left in the liquid for several days. You need to keep an eye on pot-lids in a bowl of Jenolite as if left too long, they can be damaged. Check them every day and take them out of the acid as soon as the rust has gone. Always, always soak pot-lids in water for several days after any immersion in Jenolite. If the lid has any chips or cracks, do not place in Jenolite. You can buy a rust-removing gel which can be applied on parts of the lid without totally immersing it. Your aim when dealing with pot-lids is to keep them in Jenolite as short a time as possible. Leave in water several days. If you can smell Jenolite on the lid, put it back in water for another few days.

I remember once when an American buyer bought several pot-lids from my auction. Months later, he wrote to tell me that back in the States he had displayed these on a window-sill in the sun and they had begun to disintegrate, thin sections of the printed surface lifting up. I have no doubt that this was the result of not soaking the lids in water at all or not long enough after immersion in Jenolite. (They were not my lids by the way) Where the pottery is exposed under the glaze as with a chip or crack, do not immerse in Jenolite as disintegration will take place. Use a rust-removing gel instead of the liquid. If you cannot obtain Jenolite or don't wish to use such a strong product, you can try bleach on pot-lids and printed jars, but they will still need soaking afterwards. Grey stains on lids caused by smoke from hot ashes *might* respond to bleach, but not always. Red stains on pot-lids are often proof of a brickworks lid, which has been close to the firing in a kiln and is a burn mark. These are usually impossible to remove, although bleaching can weaken the colour.

Do not be concerned about the crazing lines on the surface of a pot-lid or other printed ware, as these are a natural sign of age and are to be seen on all Victorian pottery. Only if they have absorbed brown rust marks should you treat them. Extremely stubborn brown stains may not respond after a few days, and it is then necessary to renew the Jenolite and leave to soak for another few days in fresh liquid. Fortunately most respond after a short time. Do not discard the weakened liquid; use it for pipes. And naturally, keep Jenolite, bleach or any type of acid out of reach of children and household pets.

Some pot-lids have a gold band painted on top of the glaze. This is believed to have been used only on lids which have been displayed in exhibitions, but I cannot confirm this. It is NOT usually under the glaze. Hold the lid up to the light carefully to see if it is under-glaze or not. If on top of the glaze you will naturally *not* immerse the lid in rust-remover or bleach. A gold band enhances the appearance of a lid and adds a little to its value.

When using Jenolite, you must be aware that it is a form of phosphoric acid and can be dangerous and caustic on the skin. If you wish to dilute it,

NEVER EVER ADD WATER TO AN ACID. The correct procedure is to add the acid to water. When using it, always do so near a supply of water in case of accident. If this liquid worries you, try bleach. I usually place the Jenolite and lids in plastic margarine tubs, but do not use any household bowl or basin if you will be using it for food again. Because of its expense always clean two or three lids together if possible. Use the Jenolite gel for small areas of brown stain on lids and pots. Don't forget: they will still require soaking afterwards.

LAST WORDS

I trust that I have done my utmost to pass on the benefit of my years of experience of dump-digging and collecting bottles and pot-lids. These pages have been written for a new generation of collector-diggers or even those who have never dug up some of these interesting relics. I was one of a handful of people who began in the earliest days of dump-digging in the U.K. and most of my contemporaries have departed to a better place, or are like me, are now pensioners hobbling about with a bad back.

My hope is that my words will encourage a new generation to get out into the countryside and search the places I have mentioned as you *do need* to look. Dumps will not come to you. If I were fit enough to start digging again, I would certainly search for the old dumps, badly dug years ago, by re-visiting them. They would, of course, present more hard digging the second time around.

I think the biggest opportunity today is with the private house dumps of large country houses and farms as these have remained out-of-bounds for over a century or more to all but the owners, and in most cases the present residents are completely unaware of the value and historical interest of the dump on their land. This does not just apply to owners of mansions as many farms also date from the 18th and 19th century and as they had plenty of land around them, their Victorian refuse would have also been dumped on the farm somewhere. You will need to appraise them of the facts in such a way that they become interested enough to allow you to search. Unfortunately, you will have to share the finds, but such dumps from affluent residents should be of a higher value than those of a poor family and this is compensatory. As more and more trading and housing estates are built, there will soon come a time when no town dumps are available to dig. I can see the future for dump-diggers and collectors will be in finding these tens of thousands of forgotten private dumps. They are not the kind of dumps we have been used to finding and digging, but in most cases they will not have been covered over by buildings. These are the dumps everyone has forgotten and in most cases the land-owners are unaware of their existence.

I wish you good luck, happy hunting and enjoyable digging.

Ron Dale

Lightning Source UK Ltd.
Milton Keynes UK
UKHW011827120120
356821UK00001B/45/P